John Wesley famously said 'Our pe[...]
book to help us and our congregati[...]
last few years have seen a growing b[...]
on Death from Christian authors. I[...]

of the very best, meticulously researched, biblically [...]
pastorally wise and full of humanity. Written by a seasoned
Pastor/Theologian, this distilled wisdom will help church
leaders and congregations think through caring for those
who mourn.

Paul Levy
Minister, International Presbyterian Church, Ealing, London

This author helps the Christian Pastor to understand how
to do faithful biblical ministry in light of contemporary
social and medical trends.

He speaks from the perspective of an experienced
pastor as he wisely addresses practical issues of caring for
those who are dying and their families. Perhaps the most
profitable aspect of reading this book for me personally is
the reminder that it is a privilege to be invited into people's
lives during these most difficult and significant seasons of
life and death.

Jim Newheiser
Director of the Christian Counseling Program
Associate Professor of Counseling and Practical Theology,
Reformed Theological Seminary, Charlotte, North Carolina

Over the last 20 years of pastoral ministry, one of my
greatest privileges has been to walk with Christians as they
approach the valley of the shadow of death. Situations,
questions, dilemmas, and requests from family members
can prove difficult, sometimes distressing. I am grateful to
Dr Davies for helping us think through these issues in the

light of Scripture. Written with his usual clarity, attention to detail, and pastoral warmth, this is a book that should be in every pastor and elders library.

Jonathan Thomas
Pastor, Cornerstone Church, Abergavenny,
Monmouthshire, Wales

Few things test a pastor's mettle more than ministering to the dying and caring for grieving families. At a time when England and the United States have drifted far from their Christian moorings, Eryl Davies analyzes contemporary approaches to death. His teachings about death and the life to come are biblical and clear. The author is passionate about pastoral care, and his years of ministry put him in an excellent position to offer wise counsel to pastors, chaplains, and church leaders as they come alongside those who walk in the shadow of death. Pastors will find his chapter on preaching funeral services especially helpful. *Not Uninformed* is an altogether profitable read that gives God's church much needed direction.

Charles M. Wingard
Associate Professor of Practical Theology and Dean of Students,
Reformed Theological Seminary, Jackson, Mississippi

Dr Davies lovingly and accessibly opens up for us the endless breadth and complexity of the pastoral issues surrounding death and dying, and constantly leads us to Christ our death conquering Saviour. The wisdom in these pages is biblical, gritty, real, and tested.

Tom Brand
Ministry Director,
Evangelical Fellowship of Congregational Churches

Eryl Davies grapples with a thorny subject few of us are comfortable with – death. He does so very well. Dying, death and grieving are not easily written about. This book is the exception to the rule. *Not Uninformed* is a comprehensive and compelling read from start to finish. It tackles the complex challenges many people face when confronted with the stark reality of death. Eryl Davies gives a personal pastoral perspective to difficult issues such as suicide and terminal illness in a profoundly Scriptural manner. This is an excellent handbook for pastors.

Calum I. Macleod
Minister, Ferintosh & Resolis Free Church, Scotland

Little is more seminal and challenging to the heart of any Pastor than supporting those dying and grieving. *Not Uninformed* is a gem of a book that will equip and strengthen even the most overwhelmed Pastor, in the privilege of this work. Driven by scripture and utilising many years of pastoral experience, what Eryl Davies has written is wise, sensitive and practical. The chapter on grief is particularly helpful. As the book closes, the lens widens to the challenge of pastoral care across the whole life of a church. This book will be a profitable read for any Christian with a heart for the care of those dying and grieving.

Phil Swann
Pastor, Llanelli Free Evangelical Church, Llanelli, Wales
Lecturer in Pastoral Theology, Evangelical Movement of Wales Training Course

In his immensely readable book *Not Uninformed*, Eryl Davies reviews the current secular approach to dying and death. The reader is left grateful for the significant improvements in care championed by the palliative care and hospice movement. However, he shows that these man-centred interventions fail to address key issues that make death frightening for most people. He carefully and methodically points to the God-centred alternative. A pragmatic book, it points the reader to consider how best to support the dying and their grieving families even when their faith is being tested.

In a post Covid19 pandemic period, readers of this book will learn why we prefer to argue about numbers rather than face the reality that each and every single death is a personal tragedy. We are all living one cough or sneeze away from eternity. By this bible-based approach, the reader is guided to reflect on the main issues in facing dying, death, and bereavement. Although written primarily for Christians, Pastors and Elders, this book can be recommended to all, including non-Christians who want to learn more about the alternative to the prevailing secular view.

John Alcolado

Executive Dean, Chester Medical School, University of Chester, Chester, UK

NOT UNINFORMED

SURE AND CERTAIN HOPE FOR DEATH AND DYING

D. ERYL DAVIES

Scripture, unless otherwise indicated, is taken from the *New King James Version*. Copyright © 1982 by Thomas Nelson, Inc. Used by permission. All rights reserved.

Scripture quotations marked 'ESV' are from *The Holy Bible, English Standard Version*, copyright © 2001 by Crossway Bibles, a publishing ministry of Good News Publishers. Used by permission. All rights reserved. ESV Text Edition: 2011.

Scripture quotations marked 'NIV' are taken from the *Holy Bible, New International Version*®, NIV® Copyright ©1973, 1978, 1984, 2011 by Biblica, Inc.® Used by permission. All rights reserved worldwide.

Scripture quotations marked AV are taken from the *Authorised Version* (AV).

Copyright © Eryl Davies 2020

paperback ISBN 978-1-5271-0556-0
epub ISBN 978-1-5271-0626-0
mobi ISBN 978-1-5271-0627-7

Published by
Christian Focus Publications Ltd,
Geanies House, Fearn, Ross-shire,
IV20 1TW, Scotland
www.christianfocus.com

A CIP catalogue record for this book is available
from the British Library.

Cover design by Moose77

Printed and bound by
Bell & Bain, Glasgow

Contents

This book is dedicated in praise to our triune God for the sovereign grace and joy which my late brother— Rev John M Davies (1938-2019)—enjoyed .

The Lord's covenant faithfulness was evident in making Himself so real and glorious to him, especially during the final months of his illness. It was a huge privilege to fellowship with one who knew so much of dying grace and intimate union with Christ.

Revelation 14:13

Foreword

Death is taboo. We try not to talk about it. We hide it away behind hospital curtains. And thus we are unprepared, both to deal with thoughts of our own mortality, and to confront the harsh reality of death when it strikes. Our society today is therefore, strangely, at the same time both careless and anxious. In the church, too, Christians—even pastors—are far too often unready to face 'the king of terrors' and his grim wake.

I cannot think of someone better suited to help us here than Eryl Davies, with his careful scholarship, pastoral heart, and decades of experience at hospital bedsides and ministering to the terminally ill. The result is a book that is both touchingly sensitive and robustly faithful to what Scripture has to say, reflecting the heart of the Lord who wept at Lazarus's grave and who conquered death forever. Full of deep reflection and striking practical wisdom, it is a book that will help those who grieve, those who face death, and those who minister to them.

I now have the honour of leading the ministry once led by Dr Davies, raising church leaders at Union School of Theology. How relevant this book is for such a ministry! For how a Christian faces death is the ultimate barometer of their spiritual health, and how a pastor ministers around death the ultimate test of their ministry. It is vital today that we raise ministers who can shepherd people through the valley of the shadow, and this book will greatly help us in that task.

May Christ the conqueror of death be glorified as His people are comforted and equipped by this book!

Revd Dr Michael Reeves
President and Professor of Theology
Union School of Theology

Preface

This book has a chequered history. Originally, the publisher invited me to write a book on the subject of death and eternity. Having taught eschatology to seminary students, I accepted the invitation, for I was persuaded of the need to write on this aspect of theology in a way many Christians could benefit from. After writing two chapters, the publisher was positive but suggested I may like to change the focus slightly to that of dying and death. This was unexpected but eventually I identified good reasons for accepting the suggestion and these reasons are outlined in chapter one.

I must emphasise that I am writing at a semi-popular level. I hope to stimulate readers to engage biblically but urgently with this vital subject. Church leaders are within my radar but not exclusively; many other people have shared with me their interest in the subject. After all, this matter affects us all, without exception.

While interacting significantly with secular, contemporary thought and social developments, the primary focus of this book will be pastoral and biblical. This will become increasingly obvious in later chapters. Churches need to become more aware of contemporary trends yet at the same time develop their pastoral care more biblically. For that reason, significant developments in society and medicine will be outlined in chapter two. Chapters three and four will use a Bible lens to understand suffering and death, while later chapters will move on to describe in detail the hope of the gospel, with its implications, before suggesting a pastoral care model grounded in Romans 12.

This has been a demanding project and with so many aspects worthy of consideration I have needed to be selective. Why do I describe this as a demanding project? First, it has been a learning curve in terms of understanding tensions within medicine itself and the various models employed to describe its role.

Secondly, exploring the significant development of the hospice movement, with its more holistic approach to pain and dying, has been illuminating. In addition, understanding Kubler-Ross's view of death as no more than a 'natural' event, free of any Christian influence or theological framework, was another challenge. Churches were slow to recognise this significant shift within part of the 'holistic' approach to dying with its imposition of a secular framework.

A third demand was obviously the extent of reading and evaluation involved in such a vast subject. This involved the challenge of identifying key issues to pursue in greater depth, then exposing secular ideas to the supreme authority of the Bible—God's Word. In this way, I have been stimulated and greatly encouraged, even excited, in relating and assessing contemporary secular approaches to death in the light of God's thrilling redemptive purpose in Christ.

Fourthly, there have been deeply emotional and spiritual demands as I wrestled with important aspects of dying, death and grieving. Wounds have been reopened as I recalled the deaths of close relatives and dear Christians but also read of the sufferings of others unknown to me. This has deepened my conviction concerning the urgent need to share the gospel of hope while also expressing 'genuine love' (Rom. 12:9) towards all who are in need—including the dying and grieving.

Finally, one demanding aspect of this book has been self-imposed. This concerns my passion for good quality pastoral care in churches. Readers will detect this passion in many of the chapters, so will not be surprised to find that I attempt to construct and apply a pastoral care model for churches to consider. Some churches do well in this respect, while others leave a lot to be desired—my prayer is that this book may stimulate church leaders and individual Christians to biblically reform their approach to, and involvement in, pastoral care.

Yes, it has been a demanding project but one in which I have benefited enormously in many ways. For this reason, I express my gratitude to the publishers, especially to Dr Philip Ross, for the helpful way he has encouraged me in writing this work. He has been patient and supportive and I value his friendship.

There are others to whom I am also indebted. A number of Christians have been praying for me faithfully and some specifically for the writing of this book. Their prayers have been strategic, especially at times when I struggled to find time to write or felt tired and overwhelmed by the demands of writing. In acknowledging my debt to them, I also covet their ongoing prayers.

I am grateful to one of my former PhD students, Dr Paul Held, who now works as a hospice chaplain in America. After years of missionary service, teaching systematic theology in different seminaries across Eastern Europe, he has returned with his family to his homeland. His chaplaincy work within a secular context is strategic, and I am delighted the Lord opened the door for him to engage in this ministry. I have included some helpful observation from Dr Held, and I look forward to hearing more about his ministry in the future. Gospel men who, like him, minister to so many terminally ill unbelievers in a hospice context, are at the cutting edge of ministry and are privileged, despite restrictions, to share the gospel with patients and their families on occasions. Such men need our prayers and encouragement; it is a major ministry deserving of greater recognition.

It was also helpful to discuss the subject of grief with a young Christian lady in our church, Madeleine Dutkowski, who is a professional counsellor. Our conversations over coffee were stimulating, and Madeleine also referred me to some useful resources. I am grateful to her for supporting and strengthening my pastoral approach to grief.

Finally, I thank my wife and children for their prayerful support but especially my wife for suffering many lonely hours as I wrote this book over a significant period of time. Above all, I thank our triune God—Father, Son and Holy Spirit—for His amazing covenant love and grace which alone gives meaning and purpose to life and hope in facing death. My response is well expressed by the apostle Paul in Romans 12:1:

I beseech you, therefore, brethren, by the mercies of God, that you present your bodies a living sacrifice, holy, acceptable to God, which is your reasonable service.

To Him alone be all the glory in His church.

Eryl Davies
Cardiff
February 2020

1
WHY TALK ABOUT DEATH?

Only weeks after the invitation to write this book, our family came face to face with death and future glory once again. Despite the distress we felt, the Lord graciously made this spiritually profitable for us. On hearing that our relative had just a few days to live, or perhaps only hours, one chapter was actually written in draft at the bedside during the night hours. This book, therefore, is earthed in real pastoral situations.

Although I hesitated when invited to write about death and dying, that experience was one reason that I was persuaded to write this book,[1] but it is appropriate that I share several others.

DYING GRACE IN ABUNDANCE[2]

Having pastored churches in South and North Wales[3] before training pastors and missionaries,[4] I pastored many believers on their way to, and entrance into, heaven. The memories of godly believers sometimes struggling but often enjoying and longing to be with the Lord whom they loved have lingered with me. I had heard of the grace given to famous believers over the centuries. I remember, for example, reading of Idelette—the wife of John Calvin in Geneva—who died on March 29, 1549 after years of ill-health. Her faith shone brightly in her final hours. On her death-bed she rejoiced in the hope of the gospel: 'O glorious resurrection! God of Abraham and of all our fathers, never has any believer who put his hope on You been disappointed. I also will hope.'[5]

It is moving to read about such believers but this was also true of believers under my charge. The Lord gave them dying grace in abundance, and they were 'more than conquerors' through Him who loved them (Rom. 8:37). Often I was humbled by their faith and the reality of the Lord's presence with them.

An Unmentionable Topic

Few people, including Christians, talk about death. They may think about it, especially young people, but they do not often articulate or share their thoughts. That is particularly true of men. It is almost a taboo subject in the West.

Some writers disagree. For example, quoting Geoffrey Gorer[6] that death had become a twentieth-century taboo, Tony Walter[7] proceeds to use M. Simpson's 1979 statement that: 'Death is a very badly kept secret; such an unmentionable topic that there are over 650 books now in print asserting that we are ignoring the subject.'

By 1987 Simpson could refer to another 1,700 books subsequently released on death and dying.[8] For that reason Tony Walter poses the question of whether we are witnessing a revival of death. He partly answers his question in an earlier article,[9] claiming that death is talked about much more and refers to the wide publicity for cancer research, terminal illnesses, like leukaemia amongst children, the active promotion of hospices, and the availability of trained counsellors to assist those suffering grief and bereavement. Without answering his question, Walter insists if there is a revival in talk about death then this is not due to religion or medicine but to the 'dying, dead or bereaved families themselves'.[10]

Certainly responses to death have become more postmodern and individualised, with a wide range of responses and options available, in a society which is pluralist and secularised. There is a growing amount of literature from various perspectives on the subject of death but nevertheless there remains a reluctance by many people to talk about dying and death.

Consider an article in the *Big Issue*—a magazine widely distributed in the United Kingdom, sold by the unemployed, often immigrants, in the main shopping centres and thorough-fares.[11] Caitlin Doughty's article entitled 'How to lose the fear of death' is unusual; a disturbing exposure by the young author from Los Angeles of the secretive culture and wealthy business of those who care for, and dispose of, the deceased.[12] Doughty encourages people to talk about death and prepare for it, making their wishes known to their families. Some in the United States are responding to her appeal. 'Death salons' and 'death cafes' are being opened across the country where people meet to talk about their mortality.

The author of *Being Mortal,*[13] Atul—a medical physician in the United States—also encourages people to converse concerning their end-of-life care and plan. In addition to books, considerable publicity is given to celebrities struggling with terminal cancer, as well as efforts to raise money for medical research. Almost daily our TV news brings reports of natural disaster and the carnage of wars and terrorism, while violence and death are prominent features in films and documentaries. We are surrounded by death but also the slowly increasing number of voices challenging people to think about death and prepare for it.

Challenging the Silence

An example is the growing debate in the United Kingdom over euthanasia and assisted dying. For several years parliament has discussed these issues, while pressure groups lobby politicians to influence public opinion, often through highly publicised and emotional stories of terminally ill patients travelling overseas to exercise their 'right' to voluntary euthanasia. In this context, people are challenged to talk about end-of-life issues.

Nevertheless, there remains stubborn reluctance to talk about death and Michael Henshall, the former Bishop of Warrington, confirms that 'for many people death has become an unspoken subject'.[14] In the United Kingdom, the Dying Matters Coalition of Care Organisations was established by the National Council for Palliative Care in 2009.

One recent survey undertaken by the Coalition discovered that about four-fifths of the United Kingdom public are uncomfortable discussing dying and death, preferring to avoid the subject. Approximately one third of British adults think about dying and death at least once a week, and while it has 'become more acceptable to talk about death and dying over the last decade, it remains a taboo subject'.[15] That is despite Julie Beck's statement that 'we are all going to die and we all know it'.[16] However, the fact that death is rarely talked about is understandable. We only see death at a distance on the TV and in films; rarely do people die at home but in a hospital, clinic or nursing home. When a relative dies, the dead body is removed to a mortuary or a funeral parlour immediately until the funeral.

Laura Winner is in no doubt about it, especially for the twentieth-century:

> Americans have embraced an unprecedented denial of death, an unprecedented evasion of death. In general, we have removed death from our homes. People no longer die there; corpses no longer repose there before burial. We no longer allow people to say they are dying—rather "battling" an illness.[17]

Professor Mayur Lakhani served as chair of the Dying Matters Coalition and is a general medical practitioner in England. She has given advice to medical practitioners concerning the silence over dying:

> We want to encourage people to talk more openly about dying and bereavement...we need to bring dying back into people's homes, rather than in hospital, care homes or hospices. There is a huge change required in our culture, starting with the medical profession.[18]

Professor Lakhani urges colleagues to be compassionate but direct and honest with patients when talking about dying, not offering false hopes to patients. In the United States of America, for example, Atul Gawande claims he learnt 'almost nothing on aging or frailty or dying' during his medical training; later in his surgical training and practice he felt unable to help those who were terminally ill.[19]

Cancer Ward

Solzhenitsyn captures well the negative attitude towards death in Communist Russia in 1968. A profound discussion had been in progress between some patients in *Cancer Ward*. Kostoglotov's remarks seemed to another patient—Nikolayevich—to represent an attack on a government institution. But Kostoglotov continued 'recklessly putting forward his own ideas'. Provocatively he asked, 'Why stop a man from thinking? After all, what does our philosophy of life boil down to?'

There was an immediate interruption from Nikolayevich: 'Please! We mustn't talk about death! We mustn't even remind anyone of it!'

Kostoglotov was not impressed: 'If we can't talk about death here, where on earth can we? I suppose we live forever!'

His objector was not impressed at all: 'You want us to talk and think about death the whole time?'

By this time Kostoglotov was ready to develop his point: 'Not all the time, only sometimes. It's useful. Because what do we keep telling a man all his life? "You're a member of the collective!" That's right. But only while he's alive. When the time comes for him to die, we release him from the collective …he has to die alone.'

Turning to another patient, Kostoglotov asked for a response and a 'nice geologist' replied that 'within limits that's true. We're so afraid of death, we drive away all thoughts of those who have died.'[20]

This narrative illustrates the fact that whether in Western or Eastern Europe or in America, death is often a taboo subject. I fear too that there is a silence within many Christian churches and amongst believers about dying, so there is need for more Bible teaching, alongside regular and compassionate pastoral input and honest sharing.

CHRISTIANS SQUEEZED INTO THE MOULD

I am writing this book also because of my concern that secularism is squeezing Christians increasingly into its mould so that issues relating to health, comforts, gadgets, family, money, a house, promotion, holidays, leisure, education and retirement, become all-consuming passions which are valued above loving the Lord and a firm commitment to His church.

We must care for our health and families, provide them with the necessities of life, education and a holiday, if possible. But Christians can become preoccupied with these matters and more excited by them than by the Lord Himself. Any eagerness to know and enjoy the Lord can have a low priority. By grace, Christians are heaven-bound yet too often live in the world's mould, losing the edge and zeal of their Christian lives. Consider this in relation to the elderly, young adults and teens.

Finishing Well—the Elderly
It is expected that the elderly population will grow significantly in the United Kingdom and the United States. In twenty-first century Britain, almost three million people have reached at least their eightieth birthday. The proportion of people aged sixty-five and over will jump from 18 per cent in 2015 to 26 per cent within fifty years. Currently there are more people over the age of sixty-five in the United Kingdom than those under the age of fifteen.[21] By 2031 it is likely there will be as many as 34,000 people in the UK who will reach the age of one hundred compared

with only three hundred in 1951. Current life expectancy is the late 70s and early 80s for men and women respectively. This, in turn, makes enormous demands on resources like the National Health Service. In 1970, only about 2 per cent of the population in America were aged sixty-five or over while today that percentage has risen to approximately 14 per cent. In countries like Japan, Italy and Germany, those sixty-five years old and over constitute at least 20 per cent of the population whereas China has a record one hundred million people in this age bracket!

But how should Christians end the closing years of their lives?[22] Like the apostle Paul, do we want to finish well, honouring and loving the Lord with our gifts, time, energy and resources (2 Tim. 4:7)? Most athletes sprint in the closing stage of a race in a desire to reach the finishing line. However, for elderly Christians in the West, including those who served the Lord well for years, there is the temptation to regard the days and years in retirement as a long holiday to indulge and retire from the race, even though they may be relatively healthy and mentally alert. Such an attitude suggests that Christians are, consciously or unconsciously, going with the flow of prevailing attitudes and values in society. Rob Moll is justified in advising that for many churches 'the first step' in helping the elderly and the dying is to 'rethink our vision of retirement.'[23] James Packer confirms this helpfully, explaining that zeal— even for the retired—means 'priority, passion, and effort in pursuing God's cause.'[24] Packer then quotes Bishop J. C. Ryle: 'A zealous person only sees one thing, he cares for one thing, he lives for one thing; and that one thing is to please God'.

The secular mould hinders Christians of all age groups from doing that 'one thing' of pleasing God. For example, a pastor of a growing church in Wales recently expressed his concern over the 'increasing pressures on family life. Often commitment to the church and to discipleship suffers first. Prayer is needed concerning this weakening of the foundations of Christian life.'

Teens and Twenties

For those in their twenties or older, life can be exciting but also boring, and their 'real world' is social media, relationships, leisure, sport, holidays, romance, and a career. For some, the Lord is important and witnessing in school, college, work or an unbelieving family is encouraging, but temptations to compromise abound. For example, young Christian couples who want to 'seek first the kingdom of God' (Matt. 6:33) can find legitimate but subtle, secular pressures and temptations overtaking them before they realise. Or a Christian teenager struggles over particular sins which he can both loathe and love. The question arises: is it Christ or the world and culture which fashion and govern our life styles and choices? Is there tangible evidence that 'our citizenship is in heaven' (Phil. 3:20)?

HOPE AND LIFE ETERNAL

Most contemporary literature on dying and death offers no solid hope to people, certainly not beyond death. Here is an opportunity to announce to the contemporary world that in Jesus Christ—and in Him alone—there is hope and life eternal. This note will dominate the book later. Death is not the end.

Consider the negative aspect first of all. Caitlin Doughty's work, with its attempt to remove the fear of death for people and encourage talk about end-of-life matters, is a contribution. However, she offers no positive hope for the dying. Julie Beck also discusses the subject in *What Good is Thinking About Death*. Her contribution is a sympathetic review of a sample of non-religious books on this subject that she deems worthy of reflection. Her starting point is Stoicism which became popular as a philosophy in Greece in the third century BC, then in the Roman Empire. The Roman Emperor, Marcus Aurelius embraced this philosophy until his death in 180 AD As a philosophy, Stoicism continues to be popular—pointing to happiness partly by imagining all the bad things that can happen and then expressing gratitude if they do not materialise. However, if they do occur, one needs to cope bravely with the suffering or disappointment involved, resigning oneself to it.

Beck proceeds to introduce Professor William B. Irvine's[25] book, *A Guide To The Good Life*,[26] and his advocacy of Stoicism as a path to happiness and well-being.

What follows is an outline of different theories for handling issues of life and death such as the 'terror-management' theory. According to this theory, when an individual is faced with the prospect of death he is more likely to embrace what he thinks will give him some kind of future or immortality whether it is a humanist funeral in which his life and achievements can be noted for posterity, or a scientific freezing of the body, reincarnation or religious belief. The decision is entirely personal, subjective and depends on what is more important to the individual. Beck regards Caitlin Doughty's approach as a good example of 'terror-management' and quotes Doughty to illustrate the point: But over time, thinking about death moves you closer to magnanimity. You realise that you will have to give your body, your atoms and molecules back to the universe when you're done with them.[27] Likewise, Beck's conclusion is honest but bereft of hope: 'I don't know if there is really any salvation, but if we accept death maybe we can just live'.[28]

One other example illustrates the diverse approaches to death in contemporary Western society. In a blurb to *The Revival of Death,* the publisher affirms that:

> There has been a massive revival of interest in developing new ways of talking about death. This revival, while reinstating some traditional practices and retaining medical expertise, seeks ultimate authority elsewhere: in the individual self. The new death is personal, facilitated by palliative care, the life-centred funeral, and bereavement counselling.[29]

The author, Tony Walter, identifies what he regards as 'two strands' within the revival of death. One is a 'late-modern strand' in which the feelings of the dying and bereaved can be expressed and managed, whereas the second strand involves the demotion of medical, funeral and even religious experts, in preference for the authority and wishes of the individual.[30] In an attempt to understand the complex nature of our current death culture, Walter distinguishes three types of death—'traditional, modern and neo-modern'.[31] Walter is researching the subject within a strict sociological methodology; there are interesting insights here but inevitably there is a loud silence concerning the prospect of genuine hope.

Michael Henshall captures the biblical response to the subject of dying and death:

> ...to consider death is for Christian people to consider life. At the heart of the matter is the firm conviction that God raised Jesus Christ

> from the dead. All else derived from that pivotal assertion...assurance, hope, resurrection, eternal life.[32]

The contrast between a Christian and an unbeliever dying can be powerful. For one there is a sure and certain hope while for the other there is fear and nothingness. Many examples can be given but here is one contrast, chosen almost at random.

Shortly after Alfred Hitchcock's eightieth birthday, in August 1979, Ingrid Bergman called to see the famous film director in the clinic where he was dying. 'He took both my hands', she recalls, 'and tears streamed down his face and he said, "Ingrid, I'm going to die", and I said, "But of course you are going to die some time Hitch—we are all going to die."' Then the film star informed him, 'I, too, have recently been very ill, and I had thought about it too.' For a moment, the logic of that seemed to make him more peaceful.[33] However, on leaving the room she looked back on the patient and saw fear written all over Hitchcock's face.

By contrast, almost a century earlier, Billy Bray the Cornish tin miner converted to Christ years before, had no fear of death. In 1868, just before his seventy-fourth birthday, he began to feel extremely ill. He told friends, 'I think I shall be home to my Father's house soon'. His health deteriorated further and a physician called to examine him then announced, 'Billy, you are going to die'. Immediately Billy Bray shouted, 'Glory! Glory be to God! I shall soon be in heaven.' He then turned to the physician and asked, 'When I get up there, shall I give them your compliments, doctor, and tell them you will be coming too?' Only hours before he died, a friend asked Billy if he was afraid to die. 'What?' replied Bray, 'me fear death? No, my Saviour conquered death!'[34]

Hope—it is grounded on historical facts such as the death and resurrection of the Lord Jesus Christ. This hope is not attributable to any terror-management theory but is grounded in the living, victorious Lord Jesus Christ who declared: 'Do not be afraid. I am the First and the Last. I am He who lives, and was dead, and behold, I am alive for evermore. Amen. And I have the keys of Hades and of Death' (Rev. 1:17-18).

GOD'S REDEMPTIVE PURPOSE IN CHRIST

During one of my trips to Korea (2001), I visited the Korean Demilitarized Zone (DMZ) which runs along the 248 km land border between North and South Korea, and which is 4 km wide. On each side, the DMZ is heavily militarised. I climbed a vantage point to view the North Korean soldiers patrolling their area which seemed like a stone's throw away. Nearby was Dorasan Railway Station, the most northern stop in South Korea on the rail line to North Korea. No trains leave Dorasan for the North, though the line was in place—sad but the border is closed. I use this illustration to emphasise that God's 'railway line' of redemptive history conveying His grace and light to the world runs effectively, all the way from beginning to end, from eternity to eternity. There were unique revelatory events and periods on the journey.

This unique line began when the living God—Father, Son and Holy Spirit—planned in their great love to save a vast number of people from all nations. The 'railway line' of grace operates only in and through Jesus Christ, who is the treasure and fountain of all that heaven gives to us. God the

Father chose us in Christ to be holy (Eph. 1:4), predestined us to be His sons (v. 5), redeemed and delivered us by the death of the Lord Jesus. He also gives us divine revelation and insight (v. 6-9). We are enormously privileged to have been brought by the Holy Spirit to trust the Lord Jesus and receive Him with all He has won for us, including a future 'inheritance' (v. 12-14).

But the 'railway line' of redemptive grace does not end even in heaven; it includes the cosmos too. One day everything will, in Christ, be brought to a grand finale (v. 10-11) when the Lord Jesus Christ returns personally, visibly and in glory, to consummate this redemptive purpose. The 'railway line' ends only when the entire church of the Lord Jesus is gathered together and perfected in Christ, their bodies resurrected and glorified. Simultaneously, the final judgment occurs when Jesus, the Judge, secures the punishment of unbelievers, including the devil and his host, in hell. Then there will be 'new heavens and a new earth in which righteousness dwells' (2 Pet. 3:13). As believers 'we shall always be with the Lord' (1 Thess. 4:17), enjoying Him and transformed into His likeness. Here is where the 'railway line' ends but not before.

Exciting, breathtaking, and unimaginable in its scope and future prospects. That is the big picture we may be losing sight of. One thing is clear. The 'king of terrors'[35]—death—has been conquered by the Lord Jesus Christ.

2

CHANGES AND CHALLENGES

In the 1950s, my paternal grandmother lay dying in her home in Abergele, a North Wales coastal town. Her family were called to be with her. I remember entering a crowded, downstairs room where over twenty of her close relatives stood around her bed. Death became a stark reality as I witnessed someone I loved dying. An early teenager, I saw death as an ugly, dark, mysterious and cruel visitor.

Unknown to me at the time, a new trend was emerging in society in the UK and America. More people were dying in hospitals, clinics or nursing homes rather than in their own home. Until the late 1950s, over half of the population in Wales and England died at home but this figure has reduced to under a quarter of the population. In America in 1945, most people died at home, reports Atul Gawande, but by the 1980s only 17 per cent of the population did so.[36]

Whether in the UK or in America, most people in their final hours are now more likely to be surrounded by nurses and doctors rather than relatives. This significant change has been described as the 'institutionalism' or 'medicalisation' of death, in which control lies with medical teams while others, like funeral directors, have considerable commercial interest. What emerged as a trend in the 1950s quickly became a norm.

'Parent', 'Fighter' And 'Companion' Models

Profound changes were afoot in twentieth-century healthcare. William F. May employs three helpful models to outline these successive changes in the role of the healer—a 'parent', a 'fighter,' and a 'companion'.[37]

The 'parent' model prevailed until approximately the 1950s, though no fixed year can be identified for its demise. Here the healer was viewed as the 'family physician', who cared for and knew the family well. His image was that of a parent and friend helping the family within the limitations of medicine.

The second model of 'fighter' describes the role of medicine from the 1950s as it 'shifted increasingly from a personal, familial ambience' into the 'scientific university teaching hospital'. [38] This new trend was attractive and promising, for the medical world was committed to healing and preserving human life. I wonder whether Oscar Cullmann (1902-1999), the influential continental New Testament theologian within the Lutheran tradition, unwittingly and indirectly influenced this 'fighter' model of medicine by his insistence that death is an enemy defeated uniquely by the Lord Jesus in His resurrection. Even the Lord Jesus, claimed Cullmann, feared death, seeking to be rescued from it. Cullmann's emphasis harmonised well with the 'fighter' model of medicine viewing death as an enemy to be resisted.

Nevertheless, the Hippocratic Oath[39] demanded medicine be used for improving the health of patients. Over the centuries its influence has been considerable in respecting human life and in its exclusive commitment to caring for and, if possible, healing the sick. Many continue to benefit from the research, progress and practice of medicine, while medically-assisted suicide[40] is alien to the spirit and aims implicit in the Hippocratic Oath. In a revised form, this oath is still used by some medical schools, committing physicians and surgeons to work for the benefit of patients.

Over recent decades, therefore, considerable advances have been made in providing new, effective drugs, developing innovative, complex surgery and sophisticated medical equipment—with vast amounts of money being invested in medical research. In fact, by the mid twentieth-century medicine began to 'undergo a rapid and historic transformation'.[41] Major advances meant people began to live longer as some diseases were controlled. Its success was impressive and welcome, with the medical world being perceived as powerful, if not invincible. Public expectations were now high.

The 'Medicalisation' of Death

Alongside this success, critics began to complain of the 'medicalisation' of death because it prevented patients from 'dying well'—whatever that phrase meant. Allen Verhey affirms that 'in a "medicalised dying" there is only one focus: avoiding death'.[42]

What were the other complaints? One was that dying had been depersonalised as a medical event/statistic and largely confined to a hospital. This development was inevitable for the 'experts', and their equipment were located in hospitals. The medical world was now in control of the process of dying.

Reluctance to Talk

Another criticism related to a reluctance by professionals to talk to their patients about dying. Terms such as 'very sick' or 'critically ill' were used often instead of stating the patients were 'dying'. By 1987 in England, there was evidence of improvement in this respect. For example, a random survey of adults dying in England suggested that the openness of doctors and nurses in communicating with them had improved, partly influenced by the hospice movement. The general preference for openness, however, was 'tempered by the consideration that bad news needs to be broken slowly, in a context of support, while recognising that not everyone wishes to know all'.[43]

Dr David Powell, a retired consultant pathologist and haematologist, reports that the general policy is now 'one of openness or honesty'.[44] Nevertheless, there remained too many situations of 'closed awareness' where relatives were told but not the patients, or where even relatives were left to guess the likely outcome of a condition or treatment for their loved one.

Life and Death 'Under Professional Management'

Another major criticism was the misguided, though well-intentioned mission to avoid or postpone death— almost at any cost— by means of drugs, surgery and the latest medical technology. This is the militaristic, 'fighter' image of medicine. On occasions, medical care became too aggressive, even unnecessary with distressing effects for the patient and family. The sophisticated development of high tech, coupled with new and exciting advances in medical knowledge 'led to medical dominance and power over many facets of people's lives',[45] with a domino effect on the entire caring profession.

It was in 1974 that Ivan Illich published a scathing attack on the 'medicalisation' of dying, arguing that modern medicine had 'brought the epoch of natural death to an end'.[46] When the doctor said in the 1950s that he could do nothing more for my grandmother, his consequent passive and parental role was intended to leave the patient to die naturally at home.[47] By contrast, modern medicine would have employed certain hospital procedures to ease her pain, even extend her life. My family may have welcomed that, as today such procedures may facilitate partial recovery for a significant period of time.[48]

By contrast, in 2015 a retired pastor in Wales was desperately ill at home before he stopped breathing. Despite attempts at resuscitation by a relative, he was clinically 'dead'. In describing the ordeal, the widow related that when the paramedics arrived they successfully resuscitated her husband after three attempts, then transported him to hospital where he was placed on a ventilator. Unconscious, he had several seizures until he died a few hours later. The scene was extremely distressing for the family.[49] Critics have this kind of example in mind, illustrating Illich's claim that following death's 'medicalisation', we experience our life as being 'under professional management'.[50] This is the 'fighter' model of the healer.

Dissident Voices

Already by the late 1950s doctors were expressing concern about how to respond to the dying and the role of medicine.

Medical Journals like the *Lancet* and *British Medical Journal* included articles in the early 1960s discussing ways of caring for terminally ill patients, including an openness and honesty with the patient, while respecting the patient's dignity.

Some desired a more holistic approach with new ways of caring for terminally ill patients, which included emotional, relational and spiritual needs. The 'companion' model was now emerging which led to the emergence of the Hospice Movement, the Death-Awareness movement, the MacMillan Cancer Service,[51] Marie Curie Movement, and others which provided more support for those dying, aiming to ensure quality of life in the closing stages.

Amongst the dissident voices, the following differences in approach and emphasis are significant. The literature on medical ethics complained primarily about decisions being made about a patient's care without the 'informed assent' of the patient. The literature on death and dying complained about the silence and denial of death in the culture. And the literature of the hospice movement complained about the lack of care for the whole person— the whole embodied, communal, and spiritual person who was dying when death was 'medicalised'.[52]

Dissident voices continued to express concern over the medicalisation[53] of death and there was a long historical process of identifying alternative models in order to care for the dying, while at the same time critically reassessing the role and impact of medicine.

Two of these dissident voices are now highlighted.

The Hospice Movement

One dissident voice was the modern hospice movement which surfaced in the 1950s/1960s within the United

Kingdom and the United States, challenging the growing impersonalisation in the medical treatment of patients. 'Outstanding and innovating' in this was Dame Cicely Saunders.[54] She eventually established in 1967 St Christopher's Hospice in London, which became a model for others in many locations, including the United States. Her visit to America in 1963 to lecture about her work and research on the medical management of terminally ill cancer patients impressed many people, especially Florence Wald, a nurse and social reformer. Wald[55] invited Saunders to return in 1966 to Yale as the Visiting Professor of Nursing.[56] Saunders made an 'extraordinary contribution to alleviating human suffering'[57] by her holistic approach, including physical, psychological and spiritual welfare.[58]

By combining scientific knowledge and skills with care and love, more than anyone else she was responsible for establishing the discipline and culture of palliative care[59] by introducing 'effective pain management.' She insisted that dying people needed dignity, compassion, and respect, as well as rigorous scientific methodology in the testing of treatments.[60] Wald claimed that 'beginning in the 1960s... care for the terminally ill...in the United States has been transformed'.[61]

Due to Saunders, Wald and many others, 'dramatic changes in the manner and location of care for the dying'[62] resulted in the emergence and development of the hospice movement, alongside the slow but growing acceptance of palliative care, which was gradually approved as a speciality in medicine, particularly in the UK and USA. Saunders worked tirelessly to provide, in addition to pain relief and the wise managing of symptoms, a community which was caring, open and respected the dignity of patients.

In America, hospice care witnessed steady growth, so that in 2010 45 per cent of Americans died in hospices with over half of these receiving their hospice care at home so that 'a monumental transformation is occurring.'[63.] Florence Wald saw hospice care as 'one of several patient-centred approaches that depends on more than medical science, visualises the whole person, the family, social conditions, and the soul as well as the body in its scope to understand health and disease'.

Hospice care in the United States has, however, become a complex issue, particularly with the number of private for-profit hospices which emerged. A debate continues as to whether the philosophy of the hospice has changed and whether financial profit should motivate a hospice. Wald herself complained because 'decisions about health care now use business principles', and questioned whether this approach 'will accommodate patient-centred aims and principles'. Such changes have been 'swift and without consent of caregivers or receivers of care and without government regulations' so that small hospices are 'without power'. Wald attempted to visualise a possible new order in which 'technologic medicine is separated from patient-centred health care... freeing each... to function appropriately and effectively.'[64]

Are hospice patients receiving the care they need? Are oncologists referring patients early enough to a hospice to ensure quality care? These are some of the important questions being discussed in America. Mai Hing June Mak is critical, observing that 'there seems to be little effort to examine the real situation of hospice care' in America. One example she provides is that the patients desired outcomes 'are seldom addressed'.[65] That is true to some extent in the United Kingdom but such studies are rare in

China. Mai Hing, however, refers to one study involving a small sample of thirty-three Chinese hospice patients in Hong Kong in which the researchers established what the patients regarded as the 'foremost essential element' in a good death. Not surprisingly they emphasised openness and their own awareness of dying as being extremely important.

The Death-Awareness Movement

Elisabeth Kübler-Ross's 1969 book, *On Death and Dying*,[66] challenged medicine and its methods in approaching death. Her book had a major impact yet it was not the first book to challenge medicine. Herman Feifel edited a book ten years earlier, *The Meaning of Death*,[67] while there were other books on the subject like *The Dying Patient* in 1970.[68] Kübler-Ross's book was influential because she felt strongly about ending the silence concerning death.

Robert Fulton claims that 'from the end of the First World War until the late 1950s, death in America... took a holiday. Paradoxically, the public discussion of death...was, for the most part, meagre or muted... it was considered impolite to talk about death.'[69] Others were concerned about this silence. As a research psychologist, Herman Feifel, for example, researched the attitudes of terminally ill patients.[70] Physicians were critical of his attempts to discuss death with these patients as they felt it was both unnecessary and cruel. Patients, on the other hand, were appreciative, valuing the opportunity to express and understand their feelings about death. Silence was not what many terminally ill patients desired but medical advances served to shroud the process of dying with an air of mystery and silence, in the exclusive care provided by medical and nursing professionals.

Kübler-Ross's clear and readable discussion of the subject, with the absence of technical jargon, helped to make her book influential. More important was her emphasis that death was a 'natural' event which should not be feared, along with the five 'stages' of grief which she identified: namely, denial, anger, bargaining, depression and acceptance. For these, and other reasons, Kübler-Ross was regarded as the founder of the death-awareness movement.

Considerable diversity and a lack of organisation make for difficulties in understanding this movement, but the underlying message was the rejection of the 'medicalisation' of death and the insistence that death cannot be avoided or denied, although the message that death is 'natural' was also ambiguous.

Spiritual Impoverished Protestant Churches

It is difficult to provide definitive dates, but prior to the First World War, then especially between the two World Wars of the twentieth-century (1918-1939), traditional Christian language and doctrines tended to become increasingly rejected and redundant in churches. This demise in orthodox doctrine was expressed in a more 'social' and psychological approach to pastoral work. Gradually this period of cultural 'silence' with regard to death even took hold of Western Protestantism, until approximately the late 1960s.

Culture was deeply influenced too by well-known authors, painters and film producers, like Aldous Huxley, Walt Disney and Pablo Picasso, who expressed in their different ways this fear and 'silence' about death.[71] The main character in Huxley's *After Many A Summer Dies The*

Swan lived in seclusion for years, avoiding any reference to death during his life. Pablo Picasso, the Spanish painter, sculptor, poet and playwright is one of many examples of people who did not want to hear the word death spoken in their presence. He died in 1973. The premature death of his beloved sister at the age of eight had a profound impact upon him as he went on later to live a profligate life. But within society, this ignoring, even denial, of death generally prevailed so it was not the norm to speak about it and churches were not exempt from this attitude.

Not only did Protestant Churches succumb to the 'silence' concerning death, they also failed to identify the 'momentous shift' in the new language and ideas introduced concerning dying and death by the late 1960s and early 1970s. There was a 'brand new language drawn from the death awareness movement...no one seemed to notice it.'[72] This movement imposed a psychological, secular and pluralist framework on its understanding of both dying and death, with its assumption that death is only a 'natural event'. Few churches, if any, questioned this concept, with its underlying assumptions. We need not be surprised, for at first this was a fringe but populist movement and did not operate within a church context. Furthermore, liberal theologies were becoming more diverse and radical by the 1960s, with some, under the influence of Eastern religions with their mishmash of ideas, becoming more pluralist and universalist.

A book co-authored by a clergyman and a physician even in 1936 had already underlined the changing role of the clergy in dealing with patients. The book is dated, uncritical and lacking in theological substance, but the authors insisted that with regard to the patient the minister was not a 'religious specialist'. He only had an 'advocacy' role with regard to the patient, providing a 'human presence' in a context where medical expertise ruled. This is only one example of the spiritual impoverishment of churches which contributed to a weakening of their role in preparing people for living and dying.[73.] During the twentieth century, therefore, Protestant pastoral practice in the West underwent major changes. Under the influence of 'liberal' approaches to Christian teaching, churches tended to imbibe uncritically secular philosophies and approaches with inevitable changes in pastoral practice, as well as attitudes to dying and death.

Consider an example of the influence of liberal theology on a local church. In the 1960s my first pastoral charge was a large Presbyterian church in the South Wales valley town of Maesteg. This active multi-generational church was prospering numerically but its spiritual life was at a low ebb due to years of unbiblical teaching. There was little understanding of Bible teaching, with most of the congregation having embraced critical views of the Bible. Pastorally, when I offered to read the Bible and pray with members, before leaving their homes or hospital beds, they generally declined or felt embarrassed. The minister's visit was regarded only as a social occasion and nothing more. Liberal teaching had impoverished this church spiritually, contributing, albeit indirectly, to a culture of 'silence' concerning death.

This was an 'in-between period' of 'silence' about death, which followed the era of traditional Christian beliefs and attitudes to death at the end of the nineteenth century and the early decades of the twentieth century.

Developments in Palliative Medicine

Were there changes of attitude to death and dying within medicine itself? One encouraging example was found in the British based international journal *Palliative Medicine*, which reported that during the 1990s 'there is increasing evidence that doctors have shifted from a policy of 'withholding' to a policy of 'revealing' to the patient his/her terminal prognosis'.[74] Paradoxically, however, some health workers tended to apply 'conditional' rather than 'full open disclosure' to patients. Encouragingly, in 2008 the American College of Physicians issued clinical guidelines to improve palliative care. These guidelines included support for families and carers, continuity of care, attention to well-being including existential, spiritual concerns and support for function and survival duration. Such concerns and guidelines were 'at the heart of the hospice movement' when it developed in the 1960s.[75]

Palliative care has been criticised for its increasing medicalisation but it has had a significant impact on patient care.[76] By 2002, David Clark claimed that palliative care 'has encouraged medicine to be gentler in its acceptance of death.'[77] When my own mother died in hospital seven years ago I was impressed by the wisdom and sensitivity shown by medical consultants in her care. After various treatments for cardiac and renal problems proved counter-productive, they gave the choice of continuing the treatment with no prospect of improvement or commencing palliative care. They suggested the latter, acknowledging with sadness a sense of failure, but their expertise coupled with humility and empathy was striking.

Further improvements are required, however, for Dr David Powell affirms that the 'care of the dying is still one of the neglected areas in hospitals, hospices and homesettings'.[78] In addition, Clark, with others, acknowledges the continuing tension which exists between allowing a patient to die more naturally and resisting or postponing death. Often there are no easy answers, while there are times when medical teams are under pressure, partly meeting public expectations that death must be resisted at all costs.

We have now briefly outlined the significant changes occurring within medicine, marked by the replacement of its role as parent in favour of one as 'fighter'. Medicine's huge success and progress has been welcomed by the public at a popular level. Dissident voices with their 'companion' model have provided a necessary check to the 'fighter' role for medicine but during this critical period of change, the church's voice has been weak, if not at times muted.

We turn in the next chapter to pose several big questions concerning suffering, dying, and death which trouble people.

3

Big Questions

My young grandchild loves asking questions. Her favourite question is 'Why?' On holiday recently with her parents in Berlin, they looked at part of the infamous wall built in 1961 to divide the Eastern and Western sectors of the city. The inevitable question came from the four-year old: 'Why did they build the wall?' Curious and eager to understand, questions are important for her and for us all.

You may wonder why we are devoting this chapter to asking questions. My response is that pastorally and evangelistically many people are asking questions—and lots of questions. Pastorally, whether facing major or terminal illness, bereavement, domestic and relational difficulties, or seeking personal assurance and a more experiential relationship with the Lord, questions need to be addressed. Before discussing in other chapters the big issues of life and death, we are anticipating those questions which so many people ask.

Evangelistically too, unbelievers have many questions. This strikes us forcibly in evangelising during our national

Welsh cultural festival—Eisteddfod—over the past three summers. Visitors are invited to have light refreshments in the Evangelical Movement of Wales tent but also to write questions they may want to ask about life or death, then pin them on a soft wall erected within the tent. The response is encouraging with many profound questions being posted. Some agree to answer a questionnaire, while a few visitors ask for details of churches where they can find Bible answers to their questions. A magazine is also produced each summer answering some of their questions. Interestingly, unchurched people are glad of the opportunity to ask questions and feel we are listening to them.

One reason believers or unbelievers ask questions is that we are created in the image of God (Gen. 1:26-27). God made us uniquely different with an ability to think and reason. We are rational beings, eager to understand and explore the significance of events as well as the universe. Our conscience, too, registers its approval or disapproval when we do, say, or think right or wrong things. That is why we feel guilt and shame in doing wrong, or feel comfortable doing what is right. We are moral beings created by God and are accountable to Him. A spiritual dimension also belongs to us so we are created to glorify, obey, and enjoy God. Therefore, thinking is hugely important. And it is to our minds God first addresses His Word.

Unpleasant and unwelcome things happen to us, too, and our responses include confusion, shock, anger, denial, and bitterness. The 'why' questions grip us, as well as the 'what if?' Our minds race ahead of us in an attempt to understand.

Added to this is the stark fact we can never fully understand or penetrate the mysteries of God's sovereign providence in our lives. The Bible declares: "'For My thoughts are not your thoughts, nor are your ways My ways,' says the Lord. "For as the heavens are higher than the earth, so are My ways higher than your ways, and My thoughts than your thoughts"' (Isa. 55:8-9). It is like having a few random pieces of a large jigsaw then struggling to fit them together because of all the missing pieces and the absence of the big picture. Although God provides us in the Bible with the big picture and illustrations indicating the way He works in providence, His purpose in specific circumstances is beyond our understanding. Questions are therefore inevitable in struggling to understand these circumstances and events.

Let me introduce two people who had many questions and great anguish due to so many things going wrong in their lives: Joni and Vaneetha. Their questions are our questions.

Attractive, tall, athletic and enjoying life to the full, Joni was a happy and bright teenager. Sport was important in her life as was her love of horses and horse riding. Her parents provided a loving and stimulating home for her and her two sisters. Joni's parents were strong Christians, too, and after a time of searching, Joni became a Christian as an early teenager. Before long tragedy struck.

She was only seventeen when, while diving into the sea, she felt her head hit something hard in the shallow waters and immediately her body went out of control. It seemed ages before she was lifted out and eventually taken to hospital. As a result of that diving accident, she was paralysed from the shoulders down with no control at all of her hands and legs. Despite expert medical attention, Joni was a quadriplegic and remained so with no prospect of improvement. It was hard for her and the family to accept the situation.[79]

Born in India to Christian parents, Vaneetha contracted polio as an infant and, due to a mistaken diagnosis and the wrong treatment, she became completely paralysed. To obtain better medical care, the family moved to England, then on to Canada, and finally the United States of America. By the age of thirteen, this young girl had undergone major surgery twenty-one times, so her early years were spent mostly in hospitals. By the age of seven she was able to walk but with a limp. When she was able to go to school, she was bullied.

Where was God? That was her question. Despite her loving family, she began to blame God for allowing her to suffer. It did not make sense to her. Nevertheless, she became a Christian and more aware of His love for her. Years later, following her marriage she suffered several miscarriages, then one child died when two months old. She found this 'devastating'. Aged thirty-seven with two young children, she began to suffer severe pain. Post-polio syndrome was diagnosed and it took a progressive grip on her weak body. Life was becoming extremely difficult. Six years later her husband unexpectedly abandoned her. This was 'the darkest time of my life', she confessed.[80]

If you imagine either of these ladies have been healed or freed from their difficult circumstances, you will be disappointed. Their circumstances have not changed. But they began to see suffering in a new light. They now know God more intimately and treasure the purpose He has for their lives. 'I wouldn't change my life for anything', Joni told a teenage girl. 'I even feel privileged...I'm really thankful He did something to get my attention and change me.'[81] And she means it too.

What were some of their big questions and answers?

'WHY?'

Lying helpless in the hospital and her body almost completely paralysed after her diving accident, Joni looked at her father standing by her and sensed his pain, restlessness, and disappointment seeing her in that condition. 'Why God', she asked quietly. 'Why are you doing this?' Observing the impact of her accident on him hurt her deeply. The same question cropped up often, but slowly she was learning. By the time her young niece, Kelly, died of a brain tumour, she wrote: 'I was learning that there was nothing but unhappy frustration in trying to second-guess God's purposes. Why God? Why did Kelly die? Why was I paralysed? Why was someone else alive and healthy? There was no reason apart from the overall purposes of God'.[82]

On another occasion, Joni was confused and frustrated. As she turned back to the Bible, she was reminded of the words: 'My thoughts are not your thoughts. My ways are not your ways'—'I needed to understand that', she explained, 'the Bible says our purpose is to glorify God. My life has meaning when I glorify God.'[83] The 'why' question was being addressed, but only slowly, and she would struggle with it again and again.

Overwhelmed by what had happened to her, Vaneetha also asked, 'Why? Why did all of this happen to me? If you are so loving, why did I get polio? Why have I had to struggle my whole life? How can you possibly be good?' Looking for an answer, she opened the Bible and began to read John chapter nine and the narrative about the man born blind. Did he deserve this because of his sin or the sin of his parents? His disciples wanted answers to those questions. The Lord's answer helped Vaneetha. Sin was not the reason for the man's blindness, the Lord Jesus Christ explained, but rather God's purpose (v. 1-3). God had planned it and for a good purpose. That was a shock as she had never thought of illness and tragedies in that light before. Suddenly she saw how arrogant and angry she was in the light of the sovereign God who ruled the universe. 'I will never forget it', she said, 'he had created me for a purpose—to bring him glory. And all that I had endured in my life was to accomplish that end.'[84] For the first time, she saw her own sinfulness and pride but also the right of the Creator God to do as He pleased in His world and in her life.

There were still more questions, however. For example, when her baby died, 'how would this glorify God?' 'I may not understand how,' she admitted, 'but God is doing something bigger with my life than I can possibly see.... He will ultimately use every struggle for my good and his glory'.[85]

'DOES LIFE HAVE MEANING?'

Inseparably related to the 'why?' question, this was the question posed by an agnostic, young male quadriplegic. 'I've looked at religion, philosophy, everything', he told Joni, and 'life has absolutely no meaning. It's pointless. Absurd.'[86] Joni agreed to read some of his books on Sartre, Marx and others. Their message was that life had no meaning. It was many days before Joni could reject that message, but the question challenged her deeply. Does life have meaning? Through reflecting on the Bible, as well as engaging in agonising prayer to God concerning her situation, she recognised there was a purpose, a good purpose on God's part for her—but it was a purpose she could not understand, not yet at least.

The question remains relevant for all kinds of reasons. For example, a large number of younger men in the United Kingdom who commit suicide find it difficult to perceive any meaning to life.

Here we are brought back to basics. Centuries ago, St Augustine wrote of God, 'Thou madest us for Thyself, and our heart is restless, until it repose in Thee.' [87] Joni's reading of secular philosophies like Sartre and Marx left her with more questions than answers—they did not satisfy her concerning the meaning of life.

Gannon Murphy would describe these philosophies Joni read as 'Boy's philosophies',[88] echoing the approach of C. S. Lewis. To emphasise the point of purpose in life, Murphy refers to two contemporary writers. First he quotes Os Guinness:

> Purpose can only be found when we discover the specific purpose for which we were created... Apart from such a (thing) all hope of discovering purpose will end in disappointment... (purpose) must be dug out from under the rubble of ignorance and confusion. And, uncomfortably it often flies directly in the face of our human inclinations.'

He then refers to the words of Ravi Zacharias: 'It is purpose that is prior and pleasure that must be in keeping. And let us be sure that if the purpose is wrong, then pleasure gets wrongheaded too...meaninglessness does not come from being weary of pain' but 'from being weary of pleasure'.

The Shorter Catechism sums up helpfully the Bible's teaching on life's purpose for us all:

Q1: What is the chief end of man?

A: Man's chief end is to glorify God and to enjoy him for ever.[89]

Three further questions arise from Joni and Vaneetha's experiences of suffering.

'AM I BEING PUNISHED?'

It was when Joni was home from hospital that one day she confided in her father concerning her sadness and depression—'I'm so helpless', she exclaimed. As the conversation developed, Joni again raised the question: 'But why does God allow all this? Look at our family. We've had more than our share of heartbreak.' It had been difficult for the family with Joni's accident, her sister being divorced and their young niece dying of cancer. 'It's so unfair', she said.

Her father's response was wise. He did not preach to her or minimise the difficulties they faced as a family. He was a realist and honest but humble. 'Maybe we'll never know the 'why' of our troubles, Joni. I don't know exactly how to describe what's happening to us', was his immediate response. 'But, Joni, I have to believe God knows what He's doing.'

Joni did not disagree but asked a further question: 'Do you think I deserve to be paralyzed—that God is punishing me?'

There was an immediate and resounding 'no' from her father. 'That was taken care of on the cross… but I have to believe He knows what He's doing. Trust Him, Joni. Trust Him.'[90] His answer was profoundly biblical. God does not punish Christians for their sins. He will never do that because the Lord was punished for our sins in a once-for-all act.[91] Never again will our sins be punished for 'there is therefore now no condemnation to those who are in Christ Jesus' (Rom. 8:1).

'Does it Have a Purpose?'

Joni's question and her dad's answer raise the crucial question concerning God's purpose in using suffering. There is a multi-faceted purpose. If God never punishes Christians, what purpose does God have in appointing suffering and trials for us all?

Notice the following aspects of God's purpose in suffering. A) God disciplines believers (Heb. 12: 5-11; Prov. 3:11-12). He does this because we are His children and in His family. Just as a parent lovingly and wisely disciplines a child, so God does so with His family. We should not be surprised; it is not punishment but it is for our good and growth as Christians. God disciplines us because He loves us. He is our Father whose care over us is genuine and positive. His discipline can be evidence that we are Christians—His sons (Heb. 12:6-8).

In this way, he 'corrects' and 'prunes' us (John 15:1-5) so we can be more fruitful and Christlike—an essential process for us because God is absolutely pure. He commands us to be holy as he is holy (1 Pet. 1:15-16). In language from athletics, God is 'exercising' or 'training' us (Heb. 12:11). We need to exercise faith, love and perseverance, instead of being full of self-pity, disobedience and unbelief. Although 'painful', this 'yields the peaceable fruit of righteousness' to those being 'exercised' in God's purpose. The challenge is to 'endure' such periods of discipline from the Lord and benefit from them rather than complain or become bitter.

B) Suffering and trials are used to teach us to trust, love and know God more. In 2 Cor. 11:23-28, Paul lists many hardships and sufferings he had experienced. It is a formidable list. Their purpose? To trust God rather than himself or people (2 Cor. 1:8-11). Our problems, for example, make us recognise our helplessness and need to trust God. Paul prayed for the Lord to remove his physical infirmity, referred to as a 'thorn in the flesh'. Paul prayed three times so it was important to him. It was only after the third time that the Lord answered but not as Paul wanted. 'My grace is sufficient for you', the Lord said, 'for My strength is made perfect in weakness'. Paul's response was to embrace his 'infirmities' in order 'that the power of Christ may rest upon me', determining to 'take pleasure' in all the trials he faced 'for Christ's sake' because 'when I am weak, then I am strong' (2 Cor. 12:7-10).

In God's wise purpose, the measured mix of blessing and suffering varies for us but is often how we come to know the Lord better and become more like Him. The benefits are enormous. J.C. Ryle expresses the point helpfully:

> We forget that every cross is a message from God, and intended to do us good in the end. Trials are intended to make us think—to wean us from the world—to send us to the Bible, to drive us to our knees. Health is a good thing but sickness is far better if it leads us to God. Prosperity is a great mercy; but adversity is a greater one if it brings us to Christ. Anything, anything is better than living in carelessness and dying in sin.[92]

Vaneetha illustrates the 'fruit' of suffering for us. Aged thirty-seven with two young children, her health deteriorated rapidly before her husband walked out on her; she lost her independence. There was anger coupled with depression and backsliding on her part; she also questioned

God's love for her. Slowly she was brought to her senses, finally pouring out her heart to God. She was desperate for God's help. It was 'painful' yet God was 'training' her. Let her explain:

> And God changed everything. Not by changing my circumstances but by lighting a path through the darkness. He taught me how to pray, how to ask, and how to receive. He gave me glimpses of his glory. He showed me how he is using my circumstances to change me.[93]

It remained a constant struggle, yet her testimony is that her faith has grown 'in incalculable ways' and 'one day I will see what he has done with my suffering... he is gradually transforming me into his likeness. There's no one I'd rather depend on; there's no one I'd rather look like.'

Gracious Purpose

Many Christians can share a similar testimony. Mary,[94] for example, reports she grew up on a large housing estate on the outskirts of a city in Wales. Through hearing the gospel preached faithfully at a local evangelical church she came to faith in Christ when fifteen years old. The following years included a university education, a professional qualification, a period as a tent-maker missionary. She enjoyed an assurance of salvation, a sense of God's purpose and will for her life, and His presence.

In her middle years, slowly and insidiously other things got in the way of her walk with the Lord. Mary had a high profile and demanding job and became exhausted while also caring for a terminally ill relative. The consequent bereavement and grief coupled with the almost simultaneous cancer diagnosis of another close relative added to her feelings of burn-out. A period of Christian service had also led to discouragement and disappointment but God spoke to her through her pastor's preaching from 1 Kings 19:1-18. Like Elijah, she 'woke up under a juniper tree' and 'from this point', she explains, 'the Lord had caused a stirring within me for a deeper knowledge of Him and a closer communion. It would be almost 2 years before this desire, which grew in intensity and even became a desperate desire, was eventually realised'.

Words are inadequate to describe what happened over the following months. A more diligent study of God's Word, a desire for her 'head knowledge' to become more experiential and the use of some hymns characterised her seeking of God. John Newton's hymn was used in prayer: 'I asked the Lord that I might grow in faith and love and every grace... might know more of His salvation... and seek more earnestly His face.' Her awareness of personal sin as a barrier to a closer relationship with the Lord intensified and Mary 'struggled with this for a long, long time'.

Then one morning she woke up in excruciating pain which persisted and disturbed her sleep, her life and her emotions and represented the 'dark night of the soul'. There followed a brokenness when indwelling sin caused her deep distress. God heard her prayer: 'But at last the flood gates opened and I confessed the sin in full to the Lord in prayer. I cried oceans of penitential tears and I knew the sin was dealt with.

Soon after, and through the debilitating effects of considerable pain, she says, 'The Lord showed me my self-sins of self-love/self-pride/self-resilience'. What was the result? Mary explained that in that moment of total surrender of self, 'he came in wonderful newness, nearness, fullness and power. I experienced such an overwhelming feeling of love and joy towards God in Christ and an abiding sense of peace. I was flooded with joy at entering into a tiny measure of 'the fellowship of His sufferings' (Phil 3:10). The apostle Paul makes light of loss and suffering, 'that I might know Him'. What advice does Mary give to those in similar circumstances? First, she emphasises, 'it is not just about the affliction but also about the spiritual challenge it brings... and allowing faith and love to grow in the midst of physical and spiritual suffering.'

Secondly, she reminds us 'much encouragement is needed'. How did this happen for her? 'A member of the church team became aware of the pain and maintained contact. Slowly I was enabled to be honest and share. The support and encouragement via prayer, God's Word and appropriate hymns is utterly invaluable to any soul struggling in the way I did. It was God-given help. Her pain has now reached a chronic stage with ongoing medical investigations. She concludes: 'Pain allows us the inestimable privilege of the joy of God's ultimate love. The whole experience, thus far, has brought me to the place where Christ is sufficient, even more than life itself'. Suffering indeed has a wise and gracious purpose under the care of our heavenly Father.

'How Long, O Lord?' (Ps. 13:1-2)

Although we pray, heaven can at times appear disinterested in our cries for help. At times, there is no indication God will answer our prayers. During his wife's brief terminal illness, then following her death, C. S. Lewis felt that even though he prayed, it seemed as if 'a door slammed in your face, and a sound of bolting on the inside. After that, silence.'[95]

That is exactly how Vaneetha felt. In fact, she refers to the 'agony of waiting'[96] for prayers to be answered over months, even years. Like Lewis, she felt 'God often seems silent when I'm waiting. I have no idea whether he'll ever answer my prayer, so it feels like I'm waiting in the dark'. Later, as she read the Bible and waited for prayers to be answered, she received little help in Romans 4:20-21, despite realising that Abraham waited for years for God's promise of a child to be fulfilled. But Vaneetha felt God's answer was no.

Much later again while re-reading Romans 4, she looked at Abraham's life in the Genesis narrative. She saw the warts in his life — for example, when he tried to achieve God's promise in his own way through Hagar. More striking for Vaneetha was the fact that, while Abraham was waiting, God was at work shaping his character, testing his faith and obedience as well as his patience. Over a twenty-five year period the result was that this man of faith was getting to know God more intimately. While he waited for the promise to be fulfilled, God was working and moulding his character and strengthening his faith. There was a wise purpose in the delays.

Vaneetha learnt many valuable lessons at this time and like Abraham was discovering for herself the trustworthiness of God. Waiting for God to answer prayer can make us cling more to Him and trust Him more. She wrote: 'God knows what I need; I do not. He sees the future; I cannot. His perspective is eternal; mine is not. He will give me what is best for me when it is best for me'.

That is the testimony of the Bible. Prayers are answered but not always immediately and often only after a long period of waiting. If we cherish sin in our hearts (Ps. 66:18) or remain unforgiving towards individuals (Matt. 6:14-15) and have wrong motives (James 4:3), then God will not answer. Delays in prayer are usually times when God is dealing with us, convicting us of sin or proving the genuineness of our requests and teaching us to persevere in prayer (Luke 11:1-13). In this process Christians can know God better while learning to trust Him more and enjoy His fellowship.

Job

That was true of Job—who in the sadness of losing children, servants and animals, then his own health, was plunged into darkness, searching for answers to his desperate situation. His friends did not understand either but, imagining they had the answers, criticised Job wrongly. After a long period of agonising seeking and praying, God eventually answered by showing His greatness to Job. This brought him to a more intimate relationship with the sovereign God (Job 42:1-6).

Joseph

Or think of the young Joseph with brothers who were jealous of him. They planned to kill him but modified it by selling him as a slave then deceived his father that he had been killed by an animal. Life was not easy for the young Joseph afterwards. Although he worked hard and was respected, eventually his boss's wife made sexual advances to him—which he refused. He fled from her presence then she lied to her husband concerning Joseph with the result he was imprisoned. Those who could have helped him broke their promise and forgot about him. The months and years passed by.

God's purpose seems strange and cruel in our minds. However, God's big picture was in Joseph's mind and he trusted Him despite all his problems. Eventually he was released from prison for interpreting the king's dream and appointed the chief administrator of Egypt. Even when he finally saw his estranged brothers, when desperate for food in a famine, Joseph's attitude was one of love, forgiveness and trust in God. He told them with tears: 'do not therefore be grieved or angry with yourselves because you sold me here... it was not you who sent me here, but God' (Gen. 45:5-8, 50:19-21). God's plan was so much bigger than anything either Joseph or his family could have imagined.

This is only one illustration of how God works, aspects of which we will not understand until later or until we reach heaven but God has good, loving reasons for doing what He does and when. That is why Joni at a later stage in her life responded: 'That is not to say that I now understand all the 'whys'. But I know who holds the answers, and I can wait!' In front of a large audience, she continued:

> Handicaps come in all shapes and sizes... broken homes, broken hearts, anxiety feelings that threaten to take over. Burdens of doubt. A deep loneliness. The confines of your soul may seem as limiting as a wheelchair. I know that feeling. But I also know that... God's Word is real. And... Romans 8:28 has meant...so much. And all things really do fit together for our good... and His glory.[97]

Here the *Heidelberg Catechism* confirms the truths we have underlined and does so from a wider perspective. To the question, 'What does it benefit us to know that God has created all things and still upholds them by his providence?' the answer is given: 'We can be patient in adversity, thankful in prosperity, and with a view to the future we can have a firm confidence in our faithful God and Father that no creature shall separate us from his love; for all creatures are so completely in his hand that without his will they cannot so much as move.'[98]

'Trust Me!'

This 'firm confidence in our faithful God and Father' which the Heidelberg Catechism teaches is confirmed and illustrated by Roger Abbott, who uses Mark 4:36-41 to help us understand God's ways in our lives and to trust in Him. The Lord Jesus was in a boat with His disciples as they set sail for the other side of the Sea of Galilee. A fierce storm developed and so suddenly that these experienced fishermen were frightened. The problem for them was that the Lord Jesus was fast asleep in the boat but the waves were entering the boat! They feared for their lives. In their opinion the Lord Jesus needed to act rather than delay and sleep. Eventually when they could wait no longer they woke Him. Seeing their fear, He commanded the winds and sea to be calm. The response of nature to this divine command was immediate. It was awesome to witness such a display of divine power. But there was a rebuke for them: 'Why are you so fearful? How is it that you have no faith?', the Lord asked.

Abbott draws lessons from this incident for us. Our lives, for example, can be calm for long periods then suddenly a crisis or problems emerge without warning. We are afraid. Where is God? Why is He allowing this? It seems as if the Lord is sleeping and ignoring our prayers. But the Lord expects us to trust Him at all times, even in the storms of life. Like those disciples, 'we are safe if we are with the Lord Jesus, even if He appears to us to be sleeping.' There was no need for them to panic or fear. 'The final answer from the answerer of unanswered prayer is "Trust Me!"'[99]

God certainly calls us to trust Him and cultivate our relationship with Him while also respecting that God has secrets, some of which we will never know until we reach heaven.

'WILL YOU HELP ME DIE? IS IT RIGHT?'

Those words expressed Joni's despair when, paralysed from the shoulders down, she felt dark despair. Joni was lying in hospital following surgery and felt utterly helpless. She was unable to do anything for herself with no use of her hands, arms or legs. Visitors had difficulty seeing her in that condition, often feeling awkward and uncertain what to say. Then seeing herself in the mirror for the first time since her accident, Joni screamed. It was a shock seeing herself looking so ill and thin. Crying, she prayed quietly, 'Oh, God, how can you do this to me?' Then she told her friend Jackie, 'I'm dying. Look at me. Jackie, you've got to help me.' Joni explained she could give her an overdose of pills or cut her wrists. 'You won't be killing me. You'll just be helping me die sooner. If I could move, I'd do it myself.'[100]

Despite hearing these pleadings for assistance in ending her life, Jackie was uncomfortable with the idea and refused. 'I just can't', she said, 'I want to help. I love you but I can't do it!'

There were other occasions later when, in her depression and anger, Joni begged Jackie to help her commit suicide. As a Christian, she could not agree to it. That did not stop Joni fantasising how she herself could end her life.[101] A day or so later Joni's boyfriend Dick arrived to see her. He read the Bible from James chapter one, verses 2-4 but read the verses from J. B. Phillips' New Testament paraphrase: 'When all kinds of trials and temptations crowd into your lives, my brothers, don't resent them as intruders, but welcome them as friends! Realize that they come to test your faith and to produce in you the quality of endurance.'[102]

After prayer and talking about the relevance of these words for her situation, Joni began to see there was a purpose in her helpless physical condition and she began to be more positive about it. Weeks later, however, realising she could never live a normal life and marry her boyfriend, she felt her life had no meaning. She was only existing. Once again she wanted to end her life, yet was frustrated and angry because of an inability to carry it out.

After three depressing years of suicidal despair over her paralysis, Joni writes that she prayed: 'God, if I can't die, show me how to live, please!' Joni says the 'most powerful prayer I ever offered was the shortest.'[103] It was not an immediate or dramatic change for her 'but with that simple prayer my outlook began to change.'

Suicide

There is a contemporary ring about Joni's desire to commit suicide. This is the leading cause of death amongst men in the United Kingdom with 26 per cent of them within the age range of 20-34. The rate for female suicides in England is at its highest since 2005. For young people thoughts of suicide are prompted by major factors such as acne, asthma, examination stress, rejection and bullying.[104] For others, a sense of hopelessness and despair due to circumstances and an inability to control or influence their destinies drive some to suicide. That was true for Joni. Make no mistake about it. Christians too, like Joni, can have suicidal thoughts and a few Christians do end their lives in this way. Death seems to them to be the only way out.

In the United States of America, the 2013 suicide rate was 13 per 100,000, the highest for twenty-eight years. The suicide rate increased 24 per cent between the years 1999-2014, while for males, suicide is the seventh leading cause of death. 'Suicide is complex'[105] and normally includes a disconnection and breakdown in trust between individuals, family, friends and colleagues. 'This is the most tragic of deaths',[106] yet it remains a possibility for each of us.

A suicide impacts family, friends and community in a profound way, often with long-standing feelings of shame, shock, and guilt. Families in particular can feel excluded from the private world, as well as the anguish of their relative who took his or her life. Here churches are in a good position to help, if they provide warm fellowship and a network of good pastoral support. In such an environment, troubled individuals can feel free to share confidentially with a pastor/elder or another trusted person in the church. Biblical teaching related sensitively, too, can bring hope and encouragement but only if there has been extensive and non-judgmental listening beforehand. Being reminded, for example, that life is given and taken away only by God, that all humans have worth and significance because created in God's image, that we are persons in-relation rather than isolated or independent beings, can be liberating. The facts too that life's purpose is to glorify God and enjoy Him for ever, that God loves us and His grace and presence can make a difference even in the darkest moments. This God of grace has all the spiritual resources we need in Christ.

A contemporary example in the United Kingdom illustrates the challenge of this complex social problem and the relevance of the Christian gospel. A Christian worker battled with suicidal thoughts for years. He told no one about it. If folk had known, they would have been shocked that a Christian leader struggled with the problem. But suicidal desires always lurked in the background and often surfaced strongly in his mind. Reading the words of God the Father concerning his Son—'This is My beloved Son, in whom I am well pleased' (Matt 3:17) made him long to feel loved. Mark's account of this incident is slightly more personalised (1:11) but this Christian teacher and counsellor confessed there was 'a gaping hole in my heart, in my emotions and it never got easier'.

What challenged this man reading the above words was that the Father delighted in Jesus His Son and totally accepted Him. The Lord Jesus had nothing to prove before He started His public ministry and He obeyed the Father because of their deep love relationship. By contrast, this Christian leader felt 'so unloved'. Gradually the fact that he was a child of God and the Father had chosen him but was not disappointed in him began to mean more to him. He questioned how this was possible for him as a sinner. God the Father 'is love', he realised afresh, and abounds in mercy and grace. Here was the answer to his question; 'merciful, merciful, merciful is my Father' was the glorious truth he began to understand and experience again. In this context, he spoke of the 'Father's outrageous love and acceptance of me'. However, it was 'on Calvary's hill God the Father publicly owned, loved and valued me'.[107]

The experience of this man illustrates the importance of hearing, understanding, and embracing these glorious gospel truths but also applying them to our deepest needs.

Medically Assisted Dying?

Joni's question, 'will you help me die?' could be answered differently today. Some of the states in America have since legalised medically assisted dying; so instead of pleading with her friend Jackie to help her die, Joni—if living in a state which had legalised assisted dying—she may have applied, if she wanted, to die with medical assistance.

In the Netherlands and Belgium, voluntary euthanasia would be available; in which a qualified physician prepares but also administers a life-ending drug to the consenting patient. Currently it is medically assisted dying which is receiving media publicity in the United Kingdom—with a huge shift in public support for this option over the past fifty years. Attempts to have this option legalised by the British Parliament for terminally ill patients with less than six months to live have failed.[108]

For Tom Wright[109], the campaign to secure legalised and medically assisted dying/euthanasia, albeit with specific safeguards, is being driven by a 'militantly atheist and secularist lobby'. Many Christians agree with Wright, but Paul Badham[110] disagrees and cites church leaders like the Very Rev. Dr W. R. Inge (1860- 1954) who was the 'founding father' of the British Voluntary Euthanasia Society (now renamed as Dignity in Dying). Nevertheless, Wright's more biblical objection against assisted dying is not weakened by Badham's historical appeal to church leaders who advocated euthanasia. What weakens Badham's argument is Inge's honest confession[111]—after arguing for euthanasia/suicide, he remarked: 'At the same time I hope, inconsistently perhaps, that if I were attacked by a painful illness I should have patience to wait for the end, and I do not think I should wish anyone near or dear to me to act otherwise'. This confession is unexpected as it comes from an advocate of euthanasia, but it is in line with traditional Christian teaching over the centuries.

In the face of death humans are ultimately helpless before the sovereign God and utterly dependent on Him, so the response of trust, patience and hope in the gospel is appropriate. The Church of England in one contribution to this debate suggests that 'Quite clearly suicide, and perhaps even voluntary euthanasia, might in certain cases be the expression of a refusal to trust in God, an embracing of death for its own sake, a form of self-justification, a desertion to the enemy. A final act of self-determination, whether arising from courage or from fear, is substituted for a waiting patiently in hope'.[112]

But we need to refer to three of the more popular arguments in support of medically assisted dying which we can describe as being common-sense, control or autonomy, and compassion.

Common-Sense

The common-sense argument maintains it is a reasonable option for patients who are terminally ill and in considerable discomfort, with no possibility of improvement. It sounds reasonable, especially if safeguards are maintained, but there are dangers. For example, social pressures may make a patient or family choose this as a convenient option to free themselves of responsibility for a diseased or/and aged relative. It is a 'slippery slope'—safeguards will probably be relaxed over time, allowing quadriplegics, multiple sclerosis patients and others, including those with chronic grief or simply 'tired of life', to qualify for this exit route.

Compassion

A related argument in support of medically assisted dying is that of compassion. When families describe their distressing experiences caring for relatives dying in considerable discomfort, possibly without 'dignity', we understand their desire for this legalised option. Underlying this argument may be fear concerning the process of dying and this is acknowledged by some.[113]

A preferred option, nevertheless, is palliative care[114] which has improved considerably in the United Kingdom. The Church of England contribution to the debate claims that between 1975-2000, there has been an 'experience of effective palliative care… There is almost no reason today for patients with an incurable condition to die in agony and distress'. If there is unrelieved pain and extreme distress then 'it is a disgrace for the medical profession that it should be so'. Palliative care since 2000 has continued to improve, but this must be accompanied by adequate support for the family and patient. A local church can encourage, visit and support sufferers and their families; in this and other ways the love of God Himself can be expressed practically.

Key Bible word Compassion is a key Bible word with deep significance, a word which needs to be reclaimed by the church. One major Old Testament Hebrew word is *chesed*, often translated as 'lovingkindness' or 'merciful kindness'. The word expresses God's tender, fathomless, undeserved and covenantal love to sinners in Christ who are in need. One proof of knowing this compassionate God is loving obedience to His commands (John 14:15,21 and 1 John 5:3). Genuine compassion towards the dying forbids us to support suicide or euthanasia in any form.

Control Or Autonomy

A third and contemporary argument in favour of medically assisted dying is that of control/autonomy. Joni initially hated the idea of depending completely on other people for all her needs. We understand her feelings. Toileting, washing, eating, drinking or moving her body could only be done by others. That feeling of helplessness overwhelmed and depressed her. She had no 'control' or 'autonomy', no dignity or independence. That was a major reason for asking her friend to help her die.

People use this argument in our contemporary society. Since the first edition in 1975 of *On Dying Well* was published, a second edition in 2000 observed that 'society has moved further down the road of individual autonomy and choice, often expressed in a language of rights'. However, Christians reject 'an unbridled autonomy which ignores the moral claims of others, or their own ultimate accountability to God. The primacy of individual autonomy is yet one more manifestation of the idolatry to which humankind is subject.'[115] Nevertheless, some go to the private clinic, Dignitas, in Zurich, accompanied by their families in order to be given the lethal drug. They claim the right to do as they please with their lives and die when, how and where they wish. They want to exercise control over their lives until the end. That is what they describe as dignity in dying.

However, this is a simplistic argument. To begin with, it is individualistic, ignoring the relational dimension. For example, we live in a world created, sustained and governed by the triune God. Without God the world would disintegrate (Acts 17:28, Col. 1:17), and there is no such thing as fate or chance. Wisely and righteously God governs all people and their actions without encouraging sin.

Although like Joni and Vaneetha we do not understand why things happen to us, God has a wise and good purpose. If we talk of real control then that lies with God, not ourselves. To think otherwise is to indulge in fantasy. Death is humiliating and remains a stark reality which we are helpless to stop. The relational dimension needs to be explored further. More fundamentally there is the community of Persons within the Godhead, namely, the Father, Son and Holy Spirit. The very nature of this triune

God is love (1 John 4:8) so that within this intra-trinitarian relationship love superabounds in perfect agreement and fellowship. God is not callous, indifferent or remote for His love overflows towards us in creating us in His image (Gen. 1:26), in providing what we need to live in society.

Above all, God's love shines supremely when He gave His Son to die on the cross to reconcile us to Himself. It is this sovereign God who is directing the world to its final end of 'new heavens and a new earth' when the Lord Jesus will return in glory. The 'control room' belongs to God alone. He it is who controls our lives but with compassion and wisdom.

'If Only...'

This remains true even when we make those troubled 'if only' statements. 'If only I had realised she was dying' or 'If only I had gone to see the doctor earlier, then perhaps...' or 'If only I had called to see her that morning, perhaps...' or 'If only I had gone with him then maybe...' Such statements can torture our minds, drain us emotionally, give sleepless nights and lead to clinical depression. Self-blame and guilt become dominant with such thoughts. But God is in control and nothing would have changed those circumstances.

Erwin Lutzer has helpful advice for us at this point: 'Let me encourage you to take those 'if onlys' and draw a circle around them. Then label the circle, 'The providence of God'. The Christian believes that God is greater than our 'if onlys'. His providential hand encompasses the whole of our lives, not just the good days, but the bad days too. We have the word accident in our vocabulary; He does not.'[116]

Whatever circumstances we are in and however dark the future seems; our privilege is to trust and depend on this sovereign loving God. The contemporary emphasis on rights, common-sense and compassion fuels the debate on medically assisted dying and suicide. Christians can agree with some of the arguments, so there can be common ground, yet this should not blind us to the fact that there are profound differences in terms of presuppositions, values and methodology.

For Christians, the conviction that the overarching reality of human life, indeed of all life, is God, is foundational. This conviction relates to 'God as the One who creates, redeems and brings to perfection. From him, in him and towards him men live and move and have their being... Freedom is set within a context of obedience, responsibility within a context of divine initiative and grace.'[117]

We have now addressed the main questions arising from the stories of Joni and Vaneetha but now we need to be more specific in suggesting ways of dealing with unbelieving relatives, friends and even strangers who are terminally or seriously ill or facing personal and domestic crises. Their questions are similar but how do we approach unbelievers, often unchurched, with little, if any, knowledge of the gospel? They need the gospel but how can we share the good news with them? I offer some suggestions.

Approaching Unbelievers

Negatively, a confrontational approach involving preaching 'at' an individual in a hard, detached manner is unacceptable, as is exerting emotional pressure to force a decision to 'accept' Christ. That person, whether a patient or not, can feel trapped and pushed into a superficial or even an angry response. Nor am I happy with a 'cold', detached and impersonal sharing of the gospel. Warmth, love and good inter-personal skills are essential.

Again, the emphasis is often almost exclusively on Jesus when evangelising so that people are urged 'to know Jesus'. For the unchurched and biblically illiterate, this approach is defective for it can undermine, normally unintentionally, the glorious trinity of Divine persons in the Godhead. Jesus is God the Son working in perfect harmony and love with the Father and Holy Spirit—three persons yet one God. A more trinitarian approach to unbelievers is appropriate. For example, God Himself is relational in significant ways. Fundamentally, He is relational in His triune nature with an intimate intra-trinitarian relationship between Father, Son and Holy Spirit. That relationship is permeated by, and overflows with, love and delight in one another. They are in love with each other! It is such a God who created us in love and in His image for the purpose of glorifying and enjoying Him. This is a key relationship between humans and God, a relationship we ignore at our peril.

In this context, the awareness of an 'emptiness' or 'hole' in their lives which unbelievers refer to sometimes is essentially, though not exclusively, a relational problem, because we are all created in God's image and for a purpose. Nothing and no one else in this world can fill this 'hole'— sin, rebellion and darkness rob us of what is a satisfying relationship with this living, loving God. In His abounding mercy, our triune God planned and acted to save us in Jesus Christ. He will save and gladly welcome anyone who comes to Christ. Then they will know God in a satisfying relationship which continues beyond death into eternity. If this gospel message in its trinitarian context is conveyed appropriately, it can register initially with unbelievers because of what Cornelius Van Til called 'the point of contact'—due to our being created in God's image.

Another approach being adopted in some contexts in Welsh language evangelism is 'Life—what's your story?'[118] By using a brief questionnaire, an attempt is made to 'plug into people's lives—getting people to open up about the things that are foundational to them.' The intention then is to 'show that God is at the heart of so much they build their lives on'. In some situations, with unbelievers, including those who are terminally ill, it may be appropriate to use this questionnaire and get alongside them in a more meaningful way.

Bible Verses

One lingering question remains: are there particular Bible verses or passages we should read to unbelievers, especially those facing death? Some colleagues and seminary teachers may insist on using specific Bible verses for this purpose and some are glad of that guidance. There are many well-known Bible verses which can be used, like Psalm 23.

I prefer to be flexible because people are different, as are their situations and needs. I may ask an unbeliever if they know or like a Bible verse. Occasionally they respond positively with a verse they heard or were taught when younger or which their parents used. If so, I comment on their Bible verse, ensuring that the gospel message is clear. If they cannot suggest a Bible verse, I share a verse which has helped me or someone else in a difficult situation. Normally they listen well and it can become a gospel opportunity. On the next visit, I may recap and share a related verse with particular associations which may interest them in a similar way. In this way, we can 'connect' with individuals. In prayer too, the Lord can lay Scripture verses on our hearts to share with a patient.

There was one example that stands out for me. As a pastor, I visited the local hospital most weeks. It was a small hospital where some patients were terminally ill while others were recovering from surgery or a stroke. In the male ward one afternoon, a man started shouting abuse when I approached his bed. He told me to leave him alone. I respected his wish and afterwards the staff nurse explained to me that he was a rich man dying of cancer while his wife was also terminally ill in another hospital. Their children rarely visited them or cared about their welfare. They only wanted their parents' money. Returning to the hospital the next day, the patient agreed to see me, then shared his tragic story. I listened and felt compassion. The Lord's words came powerfully to my mind and I shared them with him: 'For what profit is it to a man if he gains the whole world, and loses his own soul? Or what will a man give in exchange for his soul?' (Matt 16:26). He listened as I explained that it was the riches of God's forgiveness and peace with the holy God he desperately needed now, priceless gifts bought at great cost by the Lord Jesus, the friend of sinners. I prayed with him. He seemed reflective and friendlier as I left him. I returned the following afternoon. Sadly, he had died a few hours earlier. Those words of the Lord I had shared with him were appropriate, though beforehand I had no idea what Bible verses to share.

There is one final and big question we must ask: why death? That will be the theme of the next chapter as we use a biblical lens for understanding death.

4

Death: the Bible Lens

Leo Tolstoy's *The Death of Ivan Ilyich* was first published in Russian in 1886. The way the author weaved his sad story with its insights into Russian social life is impressive. The story slowly grips you as it focuses on the circumstances, life, sufferings and death of Ivan Ilyich, a high-court judge in nineteenth-century Russia. His lucrative position and status were important to him. He was a proud man but his marital relationship was tense yet tolerable. Promotions followed with relocation to other towns; several of his children died but two survived. Ivan hurt himself giving directions to a tradesman hanging curtains in his new apartment. The incident led to his death within a year and he soon became aware of various symptoms with pain, irritability and bouts of temper, further straining the marriage while expensive medical appointments disappointed him. The thought of dying alarmed him. Imagining work would help him, he found his professional competence was affected. He enjoyed companionship briefly with the butler's young assistant but overshadowing everything was his awareness of the blackness of death catching up on him. His final three days involved unimaginable suffering. Despair and darkness pervaded his thinking and circumstances. He died, aged forty-five.

This story resonates with us. A sudden illness, a struggle to cope with disease and the approach of death led to feelings of fear, loneliness, insecurity, depression, denial and hopelessness.[119] In such a context we are using the Bible lens to be reminded of its teaching regarding death and that is our first task.

BIBLE FACTS ABOUT DEATH

Death is inescapable. 'No one', insisted Sigmund Freud, 'really believes in his own death'.[120] A perceptive observation—in Western culture death is an unwelcome subject for conversation. It is the 'here and now' which is important, so why think about tomorrow or death? If illness does strike us, we expect to be healed or for the inevitable to be postponed for a period of time. That being so, I was still surprised when an elderly woman informed me she was not going to die. She claimed her health was good; death was not for her. Two years later I conducted her funeral! The Bible insists: 'it is appointed for man to die once' (Heb. 9:27). No one returns in a different form or an endless cycle of reincarnations. Noel Edmonds, the TV personality, disagrees: 'you can't die' for 'there is no such thing as death… just a departure'.[121] Yes, death is a departure and there is life after death, though not the 'massive, incomprehensible universal web' Edmonds imagines exists. We die physically. Irrespective of age, status, wealth, intellect or popularity, death casts its long shadow over our lives.

Death is universal too. There is no country or place in this world where you can escape death for 'death spread to all men, because all sinned' (Rom. 5:12). The brevity of human life is also emphasised (Job 14:1-2; Ps. 90:10, Isa. 40:6-8, 1 Pet. 1:24-25, James 4:14*).*

Death is also an intruder. Romans 5:12 states: 'through one man sin entered the world' (Rom. 5:12). 'Sin'—'missing the mark' of God's law—'entered (literally: 'invaded') the world'. Previously Adam and Eve enjoyed God for they were created perfect, although needing to develop in obedience; like a perfect acorn develops into an oak tree. Similarly, our first parents progress was conditional on constant obedience; disobedience would result in death (Gen. 2:16-17). The historical narrative in Genesis 3 describes the results of sin; including pain in child birth, disharmony in nature, physical death and banishment from God's presence (3:16-19). Death is an intruder.

Just We suffer for the sin of our first parents because Adam was the representative and head of the human race. That was God's decision to deal with humanity as one entity represented by Adam. Just as an ambassador represents his government, similarly, in Romans 5:12 the statement 'by one man' means that when Adam obeyed we were represented in his obedience; when Adam sinned, we all sinned in him as our representative and federal head. Therefore, physical death was justly imposed as part of the punishment for our representative's sin. However, this principle works to our advantage: 'For as by one man's disobedience many were made sinners, so also by one Man's obedience many will be made righteous' (Rom. 5:19). 'One man's obedience' refers to the Lord Jesus Christ, who throughout His earthly life and ministry obeyed His Father and died for our sin. His obedience is credited to all who trust Him.

Enemy Death remains an enemy—'the last enemy' (1 Cor. 15:26)—and in many ways; it snatches our loved ones and friends from us while death and the process of dying frighten people. For unbelievers, death is a much more powerful enemy for it leads to immediate judgment, then the suffering of God's eternal wrath. That is why the Bible emphasises that 'the strength of sin is the law'. God's law exposes and condemns us. The glorious news is that for believers, death is no longer an enemy because the Lord Jesus deprived death of its sting by keeping the law for us and suffering the punishment we deserve. There is more exciting news: 'the last enemy that will be destroyed is death' (1 Cor. 15:26). When the Lord Jesus returns, Christians will receive new resurrection bodies to enjoy the 'new heavens and a new earth in which righteousness dwells' (2 Pet. 3:13).

Looking at death through the Bible lens has been necessary because 'preaching hope is inadequate without taking death seriously',[122] but there is one more aspect of the Bible's teaching which requires attention before closing this section. The term 'death' is used in several related but distinct ways in the Bible. We have already used the Bible lens in looking at physical death, in which the union of soul and body in a human person is temporarily severed. The term 'death' in the Bible also applies, at times, to spiritual death—as in Ephesians 2:1: 'And you... who were dead in trespasses and sins...' Rather than loving and obeying God, humans are 'dead' in the sense of any desire to please, hear and love God. Not only are we sinful by nature, but we are also rebels and enemies of God in our minds and prefer to live our lives as if He did not exist. We are blind to the glorious truths of the gospel (2 Cor. 4:4), and our affections are diverted from God and obedience to a preoccupation with selfish, sinful and worldly concerns. That is why the Lord Jesus insisted, 'You must be born again' (John 3:7). Unless God radically changes us inwardly by the Holy Spirit we can never become Christians. Our desperate plight, in which we are cut off from God, is described as one of spiritual death.

Another use of the term 'death' in the Bible relates to eternal death which is the eternal punishment of unbelievers in hell[123] after death. It is physical death which is in the forefront in this book, but we cannot ignore other ways in which the Bible refers to death.

Pastoring the Dying

To call at a home or hospital or hospice where a person is ill or dying, is a privilege. Such visits can be extremely rewarding. Visits to believers also express the church's unity that 'if one member suffers, all the members suffer' too (1 Cor. 12:26). For the pastor and others visiting in such circumstances, the following advice is offered: individuals and their circumstances vary considerably. Some are more private and only want restricted visiting at their convenience. Others welcome the pastor any time and as often as he or others are free to visit. These differences need to be respected. A phone call, email or text between visits are valued by both patient and family. Visits normally should be brief unless there are good reasons to extend the time. However, do not prolong the visit unnecessarily. The patient may be glad to rest and sleep but too polite to say. Some give detailed directions to pastoral visitors concerning holding the patient's hand and what Scriptures to read but this is too prescriptive as patients are so different, while compassion can be expressed without physical contact. Being there with the patient, listening, warmly applying the Word and praying for the patient/family mean a great deal. It is essential to be a good listener on these occasions even when details of the illness and treatment are given.

This can give opportunities to be more open and gentle and avoid being forceful or aggressive in sharing the gospel. There are occasions when we need to be bold but that is different from being aggressive. One must respect the patient and be balanced in what we share. Avoid talking about your illnesses and drawing attention to yourself. Reading a few verses or a Psalm from the Bible is important and adding a brief word explaining the verses relevantly to the patient and relatives for comfort and encouragement. In some situations, this aspect may have to be curtailed because of the patient's physical condition but, if possible, include prayer, however brief.

Draw attention to the Lord's great love in Christ, His providential care and the glorious hope awaiting Christians. Terminally ill patients vary in their attitudes and responses. Listening again is important but asking a question can open the door to a deeper conversation. We should not despair if a patient is too ill or unwilling for a Bible reading and prayer. Respect their wish and return another time. It can be more difficult visiting unbelievers who are dying. Do we warn them of hell and urge them to repent?[124] Much wisdom is needed and an emphasis on the glorious love of God in Christ often gives opportunities to refer to sin and the awful hell the Lord suffered instead of us. The patient may have a range of contrasting emotions like denial, or a fatalist resignation to the illness or unfounded confidence. The freedom and rights of the patient should be respected. A tender compassionate concern for the patient and family can speak loudly in this situation. While ministering to the dying, family members need to be included in our care. The Lord is in control of their situation while the fact that the Lord Jesus wept over the death of someone He loved (John 11:35) can be comforting to them.

A hospice chaplain in the United States has shared with me some of his experiences. He meets many unbelievers in his work and observes that some feel a great need for comfort, especially at a human level. He finds this is 'one of the most difficult challenges' he faces.[125] Showing genuine compassion can give comfort but he also finds that by referring briefly to the Lord Jesus Christ, an interest is sometimes aroused. On occasions he turns to the gospels, reminding them of the compassion of Christ for people.

Pastors and Chaplains

Pastoring the sick and terminally ill is a vital aspect of the church's ministry. Whether at home, a hospice or a hospital, there are opportunities to show genuine love and share the gospel sensitively. There is need for more Christians to be involved in this type of ministry. Too often chaplains in hospitals and hospices fail to share the gospel of hope in Christ with patients. But even pastors often feel outside their comfort zone in visiting such patients and lament their lack of training or experience in this area of ministry. Nevertheless, this is a wide-open door for effective pastoral ministry.

There are differences in this type of work between a pastor and chaplain which must be recognised. A church pastor cares especially for those in his congregation or those related to members of his congregation. He will usually know his people well whereas the chaplain cares for many unchurched people who are at first unknown to him. Another difference is that the pastor's task is to share the gospel with those he visits; the purpose of his visit is social but primarily spiritual. By contrast, the chaplain has a secular employer whether private or state. Consequently, the chaplain needs to care more widely for patients and build good personal relationships by providing support. There are often opportunities to share the gospel but a chaplain needs care and wisdom in doing so. My chaplain friend points out that a pastor 'can more directly address spiritual issues without fear of rebuke from superiors provided he does not distress the patient'. The chaplain 'struggles' in this respect to find opportunities to share the gospel, unless the patient requests it. One thing the chaplain must frequently do is 'earn respect before significant spiritual issues can be broached' whereas the pastor has usually 'already established trust'. Nevertheless, my friend finds that 'the more patients/families see that I genuinely love them, the more direct spiritually I can be about the gospel.'

There are advantages, however, for the chaplain. Sometimes a patient has 'unresolved questions that s/he is embarrassed to talk about' with a pastor, so sharing with the chaplain can be much easier. Also, while the pastor is limited in the frequency and length of his visits to a hospital/hospice patient, the chaplain can be more regular in visiting and spend longer time there, if necessary.

DEMENTIA

What about dementia patients or the mentally ill, either at home or in hospital? Some of these may be Christians but communicating with them and others can be difficult.

Sometimes, visits by family or even church officers/ members to these patients can be infrequent, and visitors may be unsure how to respond to the patient. Often it is enough to sit beside a patient, reassuring and helping them drink or eat. They value company. In caring for our loved one at home, my wife and I found that we needed as a family to converse and live as normally as possible, treating her mother with the utmost respect and love, though it was demanding. As a family we often laughed at something funny that was happening to one of the children or ourselves or even the dog, but we noticed that mum-in-law was laughing spontaneously with us and seemed happy to be in the middle of family life. There was stimulation and love within a familiar social framework which she responded to at times. The family dog was also a good friend to her. Family worship held in the evening was part of the routine and, later, before her mother slept, my wife sang familiar Welsh language hymns to her at the bedside, hymns she recognised from earlier years, and often she joined in singing the words before sleeping.

We must not minimise the challenges as it is extremely difficult knowing how to respond to, and cope with, dementia patients. And there is no cure for this condition. Patience, love, respect and spending time with them are all important yet difficult, especially for close relatives, as such care in the family home is exhausting and overwhelming. John Swinton affirms that dementia is a 'brain disease, the product of brain damage brought on by a variety of different causes... This leads to serious impairment... the person will lose control of their emotions, behaviour and motivations... social skills'. The prognosis is not encouraging.

I was helped by Swinton's reference to Steven Sabat's claim that 'linguistic confusion is not necessarily indicative of impaired thinking'.[126] If a person in this condition mixes words up or uses the wrong words s/he may know clearly what they want to say but are unable to express it. This frustration felt by the patient must be appreciated and can lead to erratic behaviour on their part. I have also learned that loneliness is linked to dementia. Some medical research points to loneliness being a significant factor in developing Alzheimer's disease. 'Loneliness', therefore, 'is a central experience for many people with dementia'[127] and can be attributed partly to a shrinking social network when most of their peers and close relatives have died. Here are huge challenges for families and churches in caring for such patients. Maintaining a loving relationship, regular visits, encouraging others to visit the patient at home[128] or hospital helps in retaining a vital social network. This is where a church can contribute significantly in supporting the family by being with the patient at appropriate times.

My chaplain friend shares the fact that with such patients 'there are areas of spiritual encouragement'. For example, singing or playing a well-known hymn like *Amazing Grace* or Psalm 23 gets through to some patients. He reports: 'Several times I have ministered to dear saints over the age of ninety or over the age of one hundred, who are so confused, even thinking they were married two weeks ago, but can recite Psalm 1 or 23 word for word... they may be entirely non-communicative but the Word gets through'. He often uses the 'Wordless Book' or different variations, 'using colours to explain the gospel ... there is so much that can be done.[129]

In this respect, Dr Held is preparing a picture board so that, if the patient cannot talk, then the truths of the gospel can be communicated in colours and pictures. For unbelievers too who are patients, he frequently uses powerpoint programmes with high resolution photography of creation, such as birds and flowers, along the lines of Psalm 19:1-3. We know from Romans chapter one that God's invisible attributes are clearly seen through creation.[130] Here a hospice chaplain is exploring helpful and creative ways of communicating the gospel with patients suffering from dementia.

Dr Held also emphasises the importance of the words: 'the goodness ('kindness') of God leads you to repentance' (Rom. 2:4). Acknowledging that people are different and come to the Lord in different ways, he notes that 'kindness and sensing and attributing this kindness to God is a factor in repentance... dementia affected people... can still sense our kindness, caring, love... for example, when I get up to leave, they ask... do I need to leave so soon... they have feelings and sense our love and concern. The foundation for sharing the gospel with them then is to love them.'

But loving, visiting and caring—whether as a home carer or in other ways such as visiting—must not be confined to pastors or chaplains. The whole church needs to be involved in this ministry, although there may be some more gifted with such patients, and some may have known the person longer. Wherever possible and whatever the illness —terminal or otherwise—it is the church's privilege to care for people and encourage them in living and dying.

Caring for the Dying

Many relatives care for a loved one at home and the physical, emotional and mental strains are enormous. Their work is normally hidden from public view and few recognise the extensive demands being made on them in providing care. Caring can be complicated and relentless. 'Social care' is often necessary when the carer has full-time responsibility, including assistance in washing and dressing the patient; 'social care' also involves freeing a carer to shop, visit a friend, attend church or walk the dog in the park. These breaks are essential.

When my mother-in-law, suffering from dementia, lived with us for several years, and I was at work, my wife valued some friends from church sitting with mum and providing stimulating conversation while she had a break for an hour or two. Some carers find it helpful to attend a local carers support group to meet other carers and share their problems. Pastoral visits from church people or neighbours are therefore helpful, particularly if thought is given to practical ways of supporting the carer long term.

Nursing the Dying

Those nursing the dying and chronically ill as a profession, in hospital/hospice/nursing home or even in the patient's home, need prayer too. In common grace, many nurses show considerable compassion and kindness in their work while for Christians there is the added opportunity to express the love of God. In the United Kingdom religious pluralism and political correctness are sensitive issues requiring wisdom on the part of Christian nurses, doctors and health workers in how, if at all, they share the gospel of Christ, or even pray, with patients. They need wisdom.

Deborah Howard is a Christian working as a nurse in America caring for hospice patients either at home or in hospice. She had several reasons for nursing terminally ill patients but the major motivation was the love of God and 'the desire to live a life pleasing to Christ'.[131] The words of the Lord Jesus in Matthew 25:40 had also impacted her thinking and motivation: 'inasmuch as you did it to one of the least of these My brethren, you did it to Me'. While she reports 'there is nothing glamorous about nursing'[132] yet she presents the challenge of how we can serve others— 'how we can put their needs before our own. By our love and service to them, we are loving and serving Christ Himself'.[133] That is an urgent call to all Christians, not only to professional nurses and other health workers.

Dying Grace

For my relative who died recently, only palliative care could be provided in the final days. Death was anticipated within hours so family members kept vigil at her bedside. However, the 'few hours' extended to twelve days.

God at Work

My relative's faith in the Lord remained strong as she waited to 'be with Christ, which is far better' (Phil. 1:23). She experienced peace and when she awoke occasionally, we prayed and shared Bible verses. God was at work. On the second night, my nephew, aged forty-seven, and a covenant child, unexpectedly came under conviction of sin through words his mother had just spoken as she told her son: 'through Jesus Christ. Amen' in response to his doubts. A few minutes later she repeated the words with greater authority. Immediately her son told me: 'there is too much power here. I must go outside'. He had been with his mother for many hours so he needed to go outside for a meal and rest. Unknown to me he had suddenly come under conviction of sin. Nearly two hours later and near one hospital entrance, his need of salvation intensified so he knelt on the pavement in heavy rain, asking the Lord to accept him. His prayer was answered immediately. Grace and forgiveness were his through Christ alone. Returning to that hospital room, he related to me what had happened. It was a miracle. Beforehand he was, in his words, 'worldly, calculating and a stranger to God'. Later, although unable to say much, his mother heard him relate the Lord's dealings with him. Another night we recounted the story again for her to be sure her covenant son was saved. Her prayers over many years were now answered.

Appropriate

God sustained our relative. We became more aware of the brevity of life and the bankruptcy of worldly pleasures. The stark significance of death with the vast expanse of eternity in heaven or hell beyond death had been written indelibly on our minds as well as the remarkable grace and power of God. We had witnessed the Lord giving dying grace to our loved one who, when healthy, had expressed fears, not of death itself but the process of dying. But her gracious Lord gave peace (John 14:27); after twelve days, my relative died but the immense grief was tempered by the hope of the gospel.[134]

Economy of Grace

Dying grace is an aspect of God's dealings with His people. Some believers die victoriously in the Lord yet some may not have such grace. Dwight L. Moody, the American evangelist, was asked, 'Do you have dying grace?' He replied: 'No, I don't because I'm not dying yet!' In the economy of God's grace, He gives grace appropriate to our needs at the time. In addition to saving grace, there is restraining grace, when we are likely to disobey Him. There is restoring grace (Psalm 23:3) when we backslide openly or secretly and the Lord brings us back to Him. His keeping grace throughout our lives and in different, challenging, circumstances strengthens us to do His will and ensures we persevere in grace whatever. At the end of our lives we can trust our faithful God to give dying grace, however weak or strong our faith is.

How can Christians avoid fearing death? We need to believe firmly and constantly that our lives and circumstances are planned by a loving and wise God who supplies every need, even in dying. He does this by the indwelling Holy Spirit who uses the Word to comfort, assure, giving peace and wisdom as well as strength and spiritual reality. Our experience of dying grace will vary and may not be dramatic.

Assurance

There is comfort for believers because the Bible repeatedly underlines the fact that God wants those 'who believe in the name of the Son of God' to 'know that you have eternal life' (1 John 5:13). The Bible and the ministry of the Holy Spirit are indispensable in providing assurance to those who genuinely depend on Jesus Christ alone for salvation. Alongside the comfort, there is also a necessary warning.

Warning

To appreciate the warning, a distinction must be made between true and false assurance. In this respect, preachers and writers sometimes draw attention to the disturbing parable given by the Lord of a wedding feast (Matt. 22:1-14). Here the Lord likens the kingdom of God to a wedding feast where one invited guest was excluded because he was not wearing the required clothes. There was no excuse for the guest because the appropriate dress was also provided by the host, the bridegroom's parents. The man was careless and disregarded the condition for entry to the wedding feast. Here is a picture of those who consider themselves worthy of entering God's kingdom on the basis of being religious or respectable so they ignore the need to repent and depend solely upon the grace of God in Christ. They have no genuine or heart concern to be right with God. They are deceived. Such people must recognise that the Lord Jesus Christ is the object of saving faith and in Him alone our confidence is to be placed and certainly not in ourselves or anything we do or are.

By contrast there are many people who are self-confident and assured that in facing death all will be well with them and there is nothing at all to fear. Their assurance is not grounded in the Lord Jesus Christ. The Westminster Confession of Faith teaches that genuine assurance is for those, and only those, who 'truly believe on the Lord Jesus' and who 'love him sincerely'[135]. Such people desire to obey Christ out of love and to be more like Him in their lives which is compelling evidence of a genuine profession of faith. Preaching from 1 Corinthians 15:54-55, Charles Hodge concludes by referring to the varied experiences of God's people regarding assurance: '1. Some die in doubt. 2. Some in praise. 3. Some in triumph. It matters little, provided only we are in Christ.'[136]

Some believers do 'die in doubt' and there are many reasons for this including clinical depression and other aspects of ill-health. Or a person may be introspective with little sense of self-worth and lacking in self-confidence. This can undermine any assurance they have or had. Unknowingly, they may be imposing a form of perfectionism on their understanding of justification. This is subtle but is common to some believers who feel themselves a complete failure as Christians. One consequence may be that they are unable to believe God accepts them in His free and undeserved grace. That is not all. Christians may also hate themselves, finding it impossible to accept or forgive themselves. A compelling self-hatred may mean they are unable to look at themselves in a mirror. Their reasoning is that because they hate themselves, it is impossible to allow God to love and accept them. Consequently, instead of experiencing assurance and peace with God they are at war with themselves and plagued with doubt, even blocking any assurance or comfort being given them through the Word and by the Holy Spirit.

One believer I knew well struggled for years with doubt, fearing rejection by the Lord when he died. He was introspective, analytical and plagued with a deep-seated doubt concerning his salvation, though he was godly, loved the Word, attended church diligently and longed for a personal, deep assurance of salvation. John Piper refers to this as an aspect of 'The Agonizing Problem of the Assurance of Salvation'.[137] However, becoming terminally ill, my friend gradually experienced peace of mind which slowly replaced doubt and fear. He experienced dying grace, looking forward to being with the Lord for ever. The Lord is so kind.

LUTHER'S ADVICE: 'PREPARING TO DIE'

In May 1519, a friend of Martin Luther, George Spalatin, forwarded a request to Luther from a Mark Schart who wanted help in dealing with distressing thoughts and fears concerning death. Under considerable pressures himself, Luther was unable to respond until November that year. His response was pastorally wise in tone and detailed, while his emphasis was Christocentric. Luther had himself known such fears of death rather dramatically prior to his conversion, so he understood how the man felt. Some of Luther's advice given on this occasion can be shared. Luther began practically by urging the ordering of the man's affairs with regard to his family and work; this advice was intended to avoid misunderstandings or quarrels after his death. Forgiveness should be extended to others who had offended him but Luther also urged the need for him to seek the forgiveness of people he had sinned against, knowingly or otherwise. Luther then urged the Christian to 'Look at sin only within the picture of grace... The picture of grace is nothing else but that of Christ on the Cross... Grace and mercy are there where Christ on the cross takes your sins from you, bears it for you and destroys it… in this way you may view your sins in safety without tormenting your conscience.'

This emphasis on God's grace, on Christ's sacrifice for our sin and the need for people to 'view' personal sins 'in safety' and—for the believer—without torment is a challenge to us today. Luther then continues, explaining that on the cross 'sins are never sins, for here they are overcome and swallowed up in Christ. He takes your death upon himself and strangles it so that it may not harm you, if you believe that he does it for you... so then gaze at the heavenly picture of Christ who… for your sake was forsaken by God as one eternally damned (Matt 27:45)… there your hell is defeated… God gives you nothing because of your worthiness… but out of sheer grace… in the hour of his death no Christian should doubt that he is not alone… certain that a great many eyes are upon him: first the eyes of God and of Christ Himself… the eyes of angels (Ps. 34:7; Heb. 1:14). This call to 'view' and 'gaze' on what the Lord Jesus did on the cross for our salvation is a rebuke to many in what is often an introspective and grace-less perspective on our sins as Christians.

Luther appears to be perplexed as to how to help a doubting Christian further: 'What more should God do to persuade you to accept death willingly and not to dread but overcome it?' Here are words which many Christians need to hear repeatedly: 'he lays your sin, your death and your hell on his dearest Son, vanquishes them and renders them harmless for you… He commands his angels… to join him in watching over you'. Then comes a direct and necessary challenge to people: 'Why then should he not impose something big upon you (such as dying) as long as he adds to it great benefits, help and strength and thereby wants to test the power of his grace… therefore we ought to thank him with a joyful heart for showing us such wonderful, rich and immeasurable grace and mercy against death, hell and sin, and to laud and love his grace rather than fearing death so greatly. Love and praise make dying very much easier.'[138]

As death approaches, believers can expect our covenant-keeping God to heap upon us 'great benefits, help and strength' in approaching death. We now turn in the next chapter to consider the hope of the gospel which is guaranteed to all those who trust in Christ.

5

HOPE IN CHRIST ALONE

In his *Pilgrim's Progress*, John Bunyan describes in a vivid allegory the struggles and darkness believers often feel in approaching death and heaven. Christian is pictured travelling with Hopeful, then near their journey's end, they were able to see the Celestial City. Before reaching their destination, it was necessary to go through the deep river. Entering the water, Christian soon felt himself sinking and became alarmed. 'Be of good cheer, my brother,' Hopeful shouted, 'I feel the bottom and it is good'. Darkness, sorrow and horror overwhelmed Christian but Hopeful struggled to keep his head above the water. To encourage Christian further, Hopeful said, 'I see the gate, and men standing to receive us' and he gave several assurances emphasising that God had not forsaken them.

Excitedly, Christian shouted, 'Oh, I see him again! And he tells me, "When thou passest through the water, I will be with thee, and through the rivers, they shall not overflow thee."'[139]. Feeling firm ground under his feet again, he crossed the river with Hopeful and began to appreciate the inexpressible beauty of heaven and the great welcome extended to them.

There is certainly hope for all who trust the Lord Jesus, but how secure is this hope? That is our theme in the next section.

A. Certain Hope

This 'hope' is 'laid up' for Christians 'in heaven' (Col. 1:5). The Greek word translated as hope signifies something certain which, though future, can be anticipated eagerly; it is not wishful thinking or phantasy. The ground of this Christian hope is the death, burial, resurrection and ascension of the Lord Jesus: 'Christ died for our sins according to the Scriptures, and that He was buried, and that He rose again the third day according to the Scriptures' (1 Cor. 15:3-4).

These pivotal historical events are central to the triune God's redemptive plan. Christ was uniquely qualified to undertake this task as God-man and He actually died—'for our sins', His body was 'buried' in a new tomb, fulfilling prophecy (Isa. 53:9; Matt. 12:40) and representing the lowest stage in His humiliation. But 'He rose again the third day'. This is not phantasy for Thomas, a disciple, demanded firm evidence (John 20:27) while Paul marshals convincing evidence for Jesus's resurrection in 1 Corinthians 15:5-8. These are reliable, historically attested facts. His resurrection vindicated all He taught (John 11:25; Matt. 16:21; Rom. 1:4), while His death met with heaven's approval, securing our acceptance before God (Rom. 4:24-25). That Jesus rose physically means all Christians will one day be raised and receive a glorified body (Phil. 3:21; 1 John 3:2; 1 Cor. 15:51-57).

He is, therefore, the ground of our hope. When and how we die, where we are buried and who officiates at our funeral, or what we bequeath to families, are unimportant compared to our relationship to Jesus Christ. Death has lost its sting but only for Christians (1 Cor. 15:56-57; Phil. 3:21; 1 John 3:2).

Heaven

A sentence in a book can 'jump out'—seizing our immediate attention. That happened to me reading these words: 'preaching and teaching that do not constantly make heaven the Christian's hope and goal are not only unfaithful to the Scriptures, but rob believers of one of the most important perspectives for helping them to cope with pressures here and now.'[140] These words ring true. Often after the Christian's hope in heaven has been preached, believers may receive encouragement and joy through the message. Alternatively, in the absence of this perspective, believers can feel overwhelmed by circumstances and ill-health then lose sight of the big picture of glory. Heaven is 'one of the most important perspectives' for Christians in coping with life's varying circumstances. Consider three related aspects of heaven which can encourage Christians here and now.

Heaven for Christians Means Going Home
That is what the Lord Jesus affirmed in the most detailed statement on heaven in John's gospel: 'In My Father's house are many mansions, if it were not so, I would have told you. I go to prepare a place for you' (John 14:2). One New Testament scholar affirms that for the Lord Jesus the 'primary idea of heaven for believers is that of an eternal

home.'[141] When the Lord spoke those words, He was only a day or so away from His death on the cross. It was time, therefore, to tell His disciples even more about His death, but they became confused and distressed on hearing about it.

That is why He issued two commands in verse 1: 'Trust in God; trust also in me' (NIV). Then He explains in verses 2-4 why they should trust Him for He wanted to encourage and comfort them. Like ourselves, they needed to see the big picture. What is this big picture? It is that heaven is 'home' for the Christian. Heaven was His eternal home. He was very familiar with it. Two different Greek words are used to describe heaven here; *oikos* means 'house' or 'home' while the second word, *mone*, translates as 'mansions', 'dwelling-places' or 'rooms'. The word is also used in verse 23 and emphasises that the Christian who loves and obeys Him, enjoys a rich, mature fellowship with the Lord here because the Father and the Son have made their home with him/her. In verse two, the big picture is that the Lord is assuring the confused, sad disciples that He will be leaving them to prepare a home for them. But heaven is also the Father's home and belongs to Him. He is the One who has shown such infinite care and love towards us so believers at death are going to be with their wonderful Father.

Another aspect here is the spaciousness of heaven: 'In my Father's house are many mansions'. There is ample space for all Christians over the centuries worldwide, and no Christian will be left outside. There is more comfort here too. To banish fears or doubts Christians may have, the Lord Jesus reassures us that He Himself personally prepared heaven for them.

Heaven for Christians Means Being 'with the Lord'

A biblical way of describing the destiny of Christians when they die is that they are 'with the Lord' and herein is the supreme happiness of heaven. That was what the Lord told the repenting thief on the cross: 'today you will be with Me in Paradise' (Luke 23:43). In His prayer for His people, the Lord Jesus stated, 'Father, I desire that they also whom You gave Me may be with Me where I am' (John 17:24). For Paul, to be 'with Christ' is 'far better' (Phil. 1:23; 2 Cor. 5:8). Some Bible descriptions of the Lord's personal return in glory are breathtaking, but the climax is that 'we shall always be with the Lord' (1 Thess. 4:17). This great fact includes everything and renders everything else unimportant. There is nothing more to add.[142] Only then will the central message of God's covenant promise be completely realised: 'He will dwell with them, and they shall be His people, God Himself will be with them and be their God' (Rev. 21:3).

Yes, God is everywhere, so it is impossible to be in any place where He is not present. The Lord's gracious presence is with Christians at all times, whatever the circumstances. However, there are occasions when Christians are more aware of His felt presence, perhaps during the preaching of the gospel, or in a prayer meeting, or reading of the Bible. In times of revival there are greater degrees of the Lord's felt presence and power—with congregations and communities overwhelmed by the truths of the gospel. God's presence is real and powerful. Even more wonderful, however, is the immediate presence of God in heaven when we will see and enjoy Him fully (Matt. 5:8; 1 John 3:2).

Heaven for Christians Means Being in a 'Better Country"

That is what Hebrews 11:16 affirms: 'But now they desire a better, that is, a heavenly country.' The word 'better' in this epistle is a key word, expressing the superiority of the Lord Jesus Christ, the Son of God, over angels (1:4), the superiority/finality of Jesus' sacrifice over animal sacrifices (12:24), then the superiority of His high priestly ministry over priests under the Old Covenant. The context is striking. Although Abraham was often assured by God he would receive the promised land of Canaan (Gen. 12:6-7; 13:14-17; 15:2-6,18-21; 17:8), yet when 'by faith he dwelt in the land of promise' (11:9), he did so like a stranger in a 'foreign country'. Abraham's secret was that 'he waited for the city which has foundations, whose builder and maker is God' (11:10). This is the 'better… heavenly country' which he and other believers looked forward to.

For Christians their 'citizenship is in heaven' (Phil. 3:20), while unbelievers mind only 'earthly things' (Phil. 3:19). That is their world—the world of the here and now. By contrast, Christians by grace long to be in this 'better' country where the company is better in terms of the number of Christians there—from all ages and nations—and the quality of fellowship—with sin no longer spoiling relationships. The conditions will be better too—with the absence of disease, pain, sadness, mourning, disappointments and trials (Rev. 21:4). It is a 'better country'.

Despite his deteriorating physical condition, Dr Martyn Lloyd-Jones approached his death with a lively sense of expectancy. In late February 1981 he pointed to 2 Corinthians 4:16-17: 'For which cause we faint not; but though our outward man perish, yet the inward man is renewed day by day. For our light affliction, which is but for a moment, worketh for us a far more exceeding and eternal weight of glory' (AV). He was asked if these words described his own experience. He could only move his head to give a positive answer. A day later, he scribbled words on a scrap of paper for his family: 'Do not pray for healing. Do not hold me back from the glory.' Within three days (March 1981) he died and entered the 'better country'.

There is more to look forward to—so we turn to eschatology, with its comfort and big picture for the church.

B. 'Last Things'

'Eschatology' is a Greek word meaning 'last' or 'last things'. David Ferguson affirms that in Christian eschatology 'the four last things are identified as resurrection, judgement, heaven and hell'[143]. Eschatology is 'the final piece in the jigsaw of Christian belief' and is essentially about 'last things' and 'faith in final solutions... in the resolution of the unresolved, in the tying-up of all the loose ends that mar the life of the believer in the world.'[144]

'Two-Sided Eschatology'

While Christians go to heaven at death, this does not exhaust the New Testament 'hope'. A balance is required, so Louis Berkhof[145] distinguished between 'general' and 'individual' eschatology while Wayne Grudem[146] uses almost identical terms, 'personal' and 'general' eschatology. Carl Henry[147] referred to a 'two-sided eschatology', an appropriate phrase for expressing the inseparable relation of personal glory at death with future glorification in its cosmic dimensions. Tom Wright also seeks to redress the balance in affirming that believers at death are with the Lord 'held firmly within the conscious love of God and the conscious presence of Jesus Christ, while they await that day.'[148] Wright fails to capture the full impact of heaven's glory at death yet death 'is not the final destiny for which the Christian dead are bound, which is...the bodily resurrection … Salvation includes 'being raised to life in God's new heaven and new earth' so we are 'anticipating in the present what is to come in the future'[149] (Rom. 8:24).

GLORIFICATION

'Glorification' is a biblical umbrella term and it is important for Christians to be familiar with it. The following points describe what it means biblically: it is inseparably related to, and dependent upon, the personal return of the Lord Jesus from heaven (Titus 2:13). It is also the last stage in the application of redemption to the elect (Rom. 8:30). It deals with all the consequences of sin, including death— 'the last enemy' (1 Cor. 15:26) and the renewal of creation (Rom. 8:19-23; 2 Pet. 3:13). It will be a corporate event— all believers will be glorified at the same time together (1 Thess. 4:16-17). Included will be the resurrection of the body, Final Judgement and a 'new heavens and new earth in which righteousness dwells' (2 Pet. 3:13).

INTER-RELATED

Christian eschatology is not an optional or minor appendix to theology but 'a central Christian doctrine which conditions every other article of faith'.[150] For example, God as Creator, Sustainer, Provider, Ruler, Judge and Saviour undergirds eschatology. There is also the inter-relatedness of the Person and work of Christ, who is 'the eschatological pivotal point'[151], which has already occurred (Col. 1:19-20). He must continue to rule until He puts all enemies under His feet. This full consummation of the kingdom is awaited (1 Cor. 15:25) when Christ returns so the church lives within the tension of the 'now' and 'not yet' (1 John 3:2; Rom. 8:1, 19-39).

PASTORAL CHALLENGES

The Westminster Confession concludes by urging us to 'be always watchful, because they know not at what hour the Lord will come; and may we be ever prepared to say, "Come, Lord Jesus, come quickly. Amen."'[152] This pastoral challenge can now be applied.

First, a humble and biblical approach to the subject is required. While the Lord's glorious return will be a great, climactic event for Christians, Martyn Lloyd-Jones warns: 'There is a right way and a wrong way to study this great doctrine, and… this is an infallible test: if your study of it humbles you, your study is in the right way. If it inflates you or inflames your mind and your passion, you are studying it in the wrong way. If the study of it leads you to go down on your knees in worship… it is the right way… if your study of it makes you realise that the time is short and that you must be up and doing, that you must purify yourself and prepare…. then you are studying in the right way… This is not a subject for the mind only, it is for the whole person. It is the ultimate end of salvation.'[153] We must heed this warning, whatever our particular views may be.

Second, the Lord's return in glory demands a corporate response of alertness, preparation and wholehearted commitment to the Lord. Expounding the last words of the Westminster Confession, A.A.Hodge writes: 'God has left us in absolute uncertainty with respect to the time at which this great event shall come—in order to prevent carnal security, and to keep his people ever on the alert and constantly prepared (Mark 13:32; Matt. 24:36; Luke 12:40;

1 Thess. 5:2; 2 Pet. 3:10; Rev. 16:15).' Hodge then identifies a fourfold 'designed effect of the attitude of uncertainty with regard to the time of the second advent and general judgement.' First, 'they should always regard it as always immediately impending' but, secondly, they should look forward to it with solemn awe, yet with joyful confidence'. Thirdly, 'in view of it, be incited to the performance of duty and the attainment of holiness, and comforted in sorrow (Phil. 3:20; Col. 3:4-5; James 5:7-8)'. Finally, he uses many biblical references like Luke 12:35-37 and 1 Thessalonians 1:9-10 to emphasise it is our 'duty also to love, watch, wait for, and hasten unto the coming of our Lord.'[154]

Third, this teaching is intended to stimulate believers in their commitment to the Lord's work (1 Cor. 15:58). 1 Corinthians 15 is one of the great peaks in biblical theology: displaying the grandeur of the gospel and the certainty and implications of the Lord's resurrection—including the resurrection of the bodies of believers and consummation of all aspects of God's redemptive purpose (vv. 24-28). Here is the 'end' to which believers look forward to and anticipate with joy. Christ is victor. This big picture encourages Christians to be 'steadfast, immoveable, always abounding in the work of the Lord' (v. 58). If our work is done 'in the Lord' and in dependence on Him then it will not be 'in vain'.

William Carey

Preaching at the Northampton Association of Baptist pastors in May 1792, William Carey preached from Isaiah 54:2-3, summarising the text in the words: 'Expect great things from God. Attempt great things for God'. Plans were made the next day for establishing the Baptist Missionary

Society and within a year Carey was aboard ship with his wife and four children bound for India. William Carey took his family to India in 1793 and when the first Indian, a Hindu, came to Christ, he insisted that 'he is only one but a continent is coming behind him...We are not working at uncertainty nor are we afraid of the result. He must reign until Satan has not an inch of territory.' [155].

Fourth, church elders/pastors are accountable to the Lord in the Final Judgment as are all believers—when He will honour His people and restore universal justice. Pastors and elders are accountable for the quality and faithfulness of their ministry. I Cor 3:5-15, for example, has a primary application to them with the warning that 'the Day will declare' whether their work will bear the divine scrutiny.

Douglas Kelly identifies two motives of Paul's ministry in 2 Corinthians 5:11-16—namely, Christ as judge (v. 11) and Christ's redemptive love compelling him (v. 14f).[156] I recall an occasion when I was the target of lies and hurtful attitudes, including rejection. In that situation the familiar words of 1 Corinthians 4:1-5 came powerfully to my mind and were quickly sealed on my heart giving peace and reassurance. I was reminded that as God's servant (v. 1) I must be faithful to God above all else and prioritise on being a God-pleaser rather than a man-pleaser (v. 2). I recognised that the opinions of others were unimportant (v. 3). Like Paul, my conscience was clear but this added to my feelings of disappointment over what Christians said and did. Like Paul (v. 4), I knew my conscience was clear, though not infallible but I was reassured that 'He who judges me is the Lord'. He alone is my judge (v. 5) and will judge decisively when He returns in glory for Final Judgment (Matt. 25:31-46). There was no need to vindicate myself or wallow in self-pity. The Final Judgment is the appropriate time to judge for then the Lord 'will bring to light the hidden things of darkness', thus exposing 'the counsels of the heart'. Then—and only then—'each one's praise will come from God'.

Considerable evil continues to be inflicted on Christians worldwide; some are brutally killed for their faith while others are tortured or imprisoned. Others are targets of hatred and discrimination. Christians were amongst the millions of people killed under leaders like President Amin in Uganda, Chairman Mao in China and the dictator Pol Pot in Cambodia. A large number of Jewish Christians were amongst the six million Jews exterminated under Hitler and nearly all the Christian Jews and their assemblies in Continental Europe were wiped out by the end of the Second World War. On that day, the Judge will punish evil, honour His people while unbelievers will be punished eternally.

Eschatology is pastorally relevant, for the Final Judgment at the Lord's return is, in the words of Bray, 'the resolution of the unresolved... the tying-up of all the loose ends that mar the life of the believer in the world.'[157] The Heidelberg Catechism captures this point well with Q&A 52: 'Q: What comfort is it to you that Christ will come to judge the living and the dead? A: In all my sorrow and persecution I lift up my head and eagerly await as judge from heaven the very same person who before has submitted himself to the judgement of God for my sake, and has removed all the curse from me. He will cast all his and my enemies into everlasting condemnation, but he will take me and all his chosen ones to himself into heavenly joy and glory.'[158]

In the next chapter we will consider the responsibility of preaching the Gospel of hope in funerals.

6

PREACHING IN FUNERALS

This chapter is traditional but also controversial for it challenges contemporary trends in removing preaching from funerals and even in increasingly eliminating funerals altogether. The chapter also calls for Christ's gospel to be preached in funerals.

CHANGING PATTERNS

First, we note the main stages in the changing pattern of funerals in the United Kingdom. Peter C. Jupp identifies 'municipalisation' as an early stage in this development—for after 1850 the Anglican Church gradually lost its almost total monopoly of burial grounds. Nonconformists helped establish private cemetery companies, followed in 1900 by the Burials Act authorising local councils to establish large new but non-denominational cemeteries.

This was followed by the 'commercialisation' of funerals in the second half of the twentieth-century—so that the British undertaking industry now has a huge annual financial turnover, enhanced by offering pre-paid funeral plans. It is expensive to bury the dead. Jupp refers to 'this huge shift in powers and control over funeral arrangements'.[159]

'Consumerisation' and 'personalisation' are identified by Jupp as the next stages of funerals being affected by 'the developing spirit of individualism in Britain'.[160] What are the significant contemporary trends regarding funerals? That is our next subject.

Contemporary Trends

Preaching is not what many people or churches want, even if they have a funeral. Of course, preaching is excluded from funerals for diverse reasons, which may be personal either on the part of the church, minister or the bereaved. Preaching is minimised or omitted when funerals are a 'celebration' with emphasis on a biographical approach. An increasing number of humanist funerals are also held and for various reasons, the sign of a cross in a crematorium is frequently covered.

'No Funeral, No Fuss'

Contemporary trends are more radical. Consider the book *Please Omit Funeral*,[161] a mystery novel written by Hildegarde Dolan in which she expresses a secular approach to funerals. Two characters in her novel decide they do not want a funeral when they die. Nor do they want to attend a funeral, because everything associated with a 'funeral' is 'barbaric' and irrelevant.

Anticipating this approach, a Protestant pastor, Paul Orion, wrote a book with the intriguing title, *The Funeral:*

Vestige or Value[162] and criticised the notion of funerals being 'barbaric', tracing the idea to the counter-culture period of the 1960s with its denial of death. For Orion, fear is at the root of this denial which constitutes an 'irrational' philosophy. Orion's message is that the funeral can comfort bereaved relatives and friends if it addresses relevant and important theological, social and psychological aspects.

This trend which Orion criticised was certainly not confined to the late twentieth-century—remaining deeply entrenched in contemporary Western society today. Think of the intriguing title of a newspaper article by Rosemary Bennett: 'No funeral, no fuss: the modern send-off'.[163] She reports that traditional funerals and family gatherings are 'becoming increasingly rare' because more folk desire a 'minimum fuss send-off' and therefore arrange for 'direct cremation' in which the deceased is removed from a hospital or another location as soon as possible to a crematorium, without a funeral or service or even relatives present. The ashes may be scattered by the funeral director without family being there. About two thousand people annually choose direct cremation in Britain, reducing the cost by two-thirds. In some situations, a 'celebration' of the deceased person's life may be held later but without mourning or references to death.

Introduced to the United Kingdom a couple of decades ago, Simplicita Cremations have about three hundred clients per year. Their clients are usually professionals wanting a send-off which is personal, non-traditional and protects families from unnecessary emotional pressures. For some reaching old age and possibly facing terminal/degenerative diseases, death is viewed as a relief. The direct, impersonal disposal of the body is convenient, not requiring family involvement. Relatives can therefore celebrate or just continue their lives, rather than mourn.

COMPLEX

One significant development in the United Kingdom and America is that of Civil Celebrants who are non-clergy professionals. [164] These are 'neutral' and not linked formally to, or representing, any religion, group or system of belief. There are no legal requirements to become Celebrants but they are expected to have a clean, smart appearance, a pleasing personality, inter-personal skills, good diction, an ability to speak publicly, as well as IT skills. Training is provided with separate training courses both for weddings and funerals. These short courses can be followed online or in classes.[165] Basically their role is to conduct 'people-centred ceremonies' in consultation with bereaved families who expect 'tailored' services which they or the deceased have suggested.

The absence of preaching and Christian influence makes it a secular, client-orientated approach to funerals; professional clergy/churches may soon have only a minor role.

CHURCH FUNERALS

What is the contemporary situation in Protestant churches regarding funerals? One Christian friend, retired from the funeral industry, gave me his observations. He found that in Protestant churches there is little preaching. If there is preaching, it is brief but often lacking biblical content. People are regarded as 'nice' or 'good', with everyone arriving in 'heaven' irrespective of faith or life-style.

A frequently used illustration in these funerals is that of a boat leaving the harbour. Death is only leaving the harbour of this world to commence a journey with no indication concerning the nature, destination or duration of the journey.

In two funerals I attended, both conducted by Free Church ministers belonging to major denominations, the minister who prayed did not refer to Jesus Christ once. Nor did the other minister refer to the Christian gospel in his 'message'. On both occasions the 'message' was biographical. It was not a Christian funeral in any sense.

My friend commented more favourably concerning funerals in evangelical and Pentecostal churches in South Wales. He reported that gospel preaching occurs in these funerals, although varying in quality, length, suitability and gospel content. In one Pentecostal church, warmth radiated from the pastor and congregation with the gospel hope communicated sensitively and lovingly. By contrast, in a few funerals in Reformed churches no reference was made to the deceased or the bereaved family; there was a complete disconnect between preacher and the bereaved, though the gospel was preached.

Safeguards

There were safeguards I established as pastor to secure preaching in funerals. One was to ensure it was a Christian service with strict limits on the time for tributes/poetry if requested. I preferred to gather information from the family and briefly share it myself, prior to preaching. Another pressure was ensuring adequate time for the service and preaching. Too often there is an unnecessarily tight, inadequate schedule, so time spent discussing arrangements with relatives and the funeral director was well spent.

There were other pressures too. Occasionally, there was a request from a 'secret' social organization to participate in the service or commital. Imagine my surprise as I waited to enter a crematorium with mourners when an organisation asked me for a five-minute pause before the committal for their ritual, including dancing around the coffin. His consternation was visible on hearing my firm refusal! The extensive absence of gospel preaching in funeral services in the United Kingdom is sad.

America

The situation in America is similar but complex. One American pastoral theologian reports that 'many pastors today are aware... that funeral practices have drifted off course', with blame attributed to the funeral commercial 'industry' for moving funerals away from the church. That, however, is a superficial response for 'it is we ourselves, as pastors and pastoral theologians, who have co-operated with cultural trends around us and done much to weaken the Christian funeral.'[166] The professor reports that funerals in America 'are indeed changing', indicating a 'shift in our theology'.[167] Consequently, funerals are 'more upbeat, more filled with laughter, more festive' and 'tend to be less formal, less governed by ritual, more relaxed and personal'. With regard to preaching in funerals, there is 'much confusion'. Preachers in funerals can be torn between giving anecdotes, providing a fleeting reference to a Bible verse or delivering a lengthy message.

But then, 'is a sermon at a funeral necessary?'[168] The answer will become apparent but here I am only identifying contemporary trends and underlining the confusion existing in churches concerning what constitutes a Christian funeral.

Significance of a Funeral

What is the significance of a funeral service? A funeral can be helpful in offering closure for the family with regard to their deceased relative. This can be a valuable, even necessary, reason for holding a funeral as it assists the process of grieving, in bringing about acceptance of the death, including a final farewell. Penelope Wilcock agrees that the funeral 'is a vital ingredient in the process of separation from the dead. It is often the first point of moving on from the numbness of shock and disbelief' and 'often allows this work (of grief) to begin… it is almost invariably a landmark of significance.'[169] To confirm this point, Derek Nuttall suggests that in bereavement we are 'entering more deeply into a time of transition and significantly without the person with whom we may have shared previous life changes. Like other major transitions in life, birth, growing up, marriage, divorce, retirement, a rite of passage is needed to mark it and help us through it.'[170] Again for mourners, hearing the Word of God read then preached in a caring, prayerful context can be a source of immense comfort and reassurance.

A funeral also provides an opportunity for church and friends to identify with mourners publicly in expressions of love, prayer and practical support which hopefully continue beyond the funeral. Derek Nuttall underlines this benefit: 'Those who are bereaved need to know that the one who has died mattered to others and will be missed by others.'[171] A funeral service can also contribute to the church's spiritual life in challenging and restoring Christians, even moving the church out of any complacency.

A final point needs to be made concerning the significance of a funeral. Robert Grainger claims that 'funerals are a clear assertion that death, like life, is in God's hands'.[172] And death speaks in various ways to us. God used a funeral service when an elderly Christian woman in the church I pastored died: during the funeral service a fifty-three year-old man who had backslidden for years was brought back to the Lord. For years afterwards, he became a stalwart in the church and a strong witness to the gospel. Sometimes individuals are converted as a result of a funeral service, too. Such a service has huge potential for good for the bereaved, their friends and the church.

Preaching in Funerals

Charles Hoffacker understands my experience of preaching in funerals: 'The role of funeral preacher challenges and stretches the pastor no matter how many funerals he or she has taken before.'[173] What are these challenges? There are pastoral demands visiting the bereaved. In 'difficult' funerals like the death of a child, a teenager or a young mother snatched from her husband and children, there are huge emotional pressures which can overcome the pastor. It happened to me on occasions and I was 'stretched'. There can be pressures too in co-ordinating arrangements or preaching to a mixed congregation of believers/unbelievers, with the additional need to pray for the family. Churches need to pray for pastors in these situations.

POINTERS

How should we approach the task of preaching in funerals? I offer three major pointers, namely: drama, declaration and discipline.

1. DRAMA

Yes, drama! The gospel is essentially dramatic, speaking of the coming of God's Son to earth. Following His perfect life, miracles, and teaching—revealing God the Father—He died for our sin, rose triumphantly from the dead and ascended to the Father in heaven. He had won forgiveness and eternal life for us—conquering death, hell and Satan. He is victor and Lord over all. That is a unique, remarkable drama which people need to hear. This is the meta-narrative, and we now anticipate His return in glory.

Our preaching at all times, including funeral preaching, needs to reflect this exciting drama. To describe the gospel, Kevin J. Vanhoozer uses the helpful term 'theo-dramatic',[174] emphasising 'a series of divine entrances and exits, especially as these pertain to what God has done in Jesus Christ'. This drama model focuses on 'the centrality of communicative action, both human and divine' and 'stretches' the preacher.[175]

There are two interrelated aspects to this drama which demand our brief attention. One is the drama taking place in the family suffering bereavement. Sometimes the dramatic aspect may be especially tragic in the cause and suddenness of death or its impact on the family. Possibly their intense grief and despair may be overwhelming or there may be strained relationships within the family being played out. Pastors may not be privy to all these details but in almost all funerals, whether quietly or openly, a drama of varying kinds is in progress in the bereaved family.

The second related aspect is the drama occurring when in the funeral service through reading and preaching the Word, eternity impacts the complex attitudes, responses and relationships of family members. This aspect of the drama is outside our control. It is the work of God's Spirit—no human can penetrate and change their hearts or lives. Preachers and churches, therefore, should pray for God to intervene radically in people's lives. The potential for blessing is enormous. The Holy Spirit's work is to apply the Word powerfully to the consciences and hearts of individuals. This aspect of the drama is exciting, even surprising.

Unexpected
On occasion, the response is unexpected, even disturbing. Eight years ago, I preached in the funeral of an elderly lady, using John 3:16, sensitively and briefly. It was obvious some relatives were angry as they listened to the gospel. Outside the funeral home afterwards and ready to go to the graveside, one son angrily blamed me for preaching like that and 'offending' them. Holding my jacket and tie, he shouted his anger in front of the mourners and was about to hit me when the funeral director intervened. Drama!

That can be involved in the drama of proclaiming the living Word of God which for hearers is either 'the aroma of death leading to death' or to the other 'the aroma of life leading to life' (2 Cor. 2:16).

2. DECLARATION

In our postmodern context 'truth' is viewed as being relative, subjectively determined by individuals. By contrast, preaching must objectively declare revealed truths and historically attested facts. There are three ways in which preaching as declaration can be strengthened in funerals today.

Authoritative

One way is by ensuring our preaching is authoritative. I am not referring to the preacher's personality, eloquence, learning or status, which can impress people. Vanhoozer captures the point: 'to preach is to address people in God's name' which involves expounding and applying the objective, written Word of God, rather than expressing our ideas or feelings. I want a counter-cultural approach which refuses to pay homage to 'truth-decay' and the deconstruction of biblical truths into language games in which 'the very idea of absolute and universal truth is considered implausible, held in open contempt or not even seriously considered'.[176] Rather, 'the word of the Lord endures forever' (1 Pet. 1:25). The divine, objectively revealed Word of God 'lives and abides forever' (v. 23); 'truth-decay' is a lie!

An authoritative declaration of the gospel with its central meta-narrative is essential. 'Without truth,' warns Dennis McCallum, 'Christianity itself will vanish or be swallowed up in an ocean of subjective religious experience'[177] or a mishmash of ideas that is occurring in Western Christendom. The preacher's authority derives from God's Word and extends only so far as the preacher proclaims the biblical text with its meta-narrative. That is true when preaching in funerals, where it is a temptation to be weaker on the Christ-centred meta-narrative in favour of anecdotes or 'devotional', sentimental comments.

Authority in preaching is related inseparably to God's self-revelation in His Word. Calvin reminds us that 'God does not speak openly from heaven, but employs men as his instruments, that by their agency he may make known his will'.[178] Consequently, when His Word is proclaimed faithfully, 'there God's voice ringeth in our ears'[179] for God 'does not wish to be heard but by the voice of his minister'.[180] That 'stretches' preachers further in terms of responsibility.

Accessible

A second way in which preaching as declaration can be developed is by making it accessible. Preaching must communicate clearly and connect with mourners—building a bridge for the preacher to bring the riches of the Word into the listeners' world. Charles Hoffacker suggests the idea of 'finding the key' and regards the period between the death of a person and the burial/cremation as a demanding time for preacher and mourners.[181] The preacher's contact with the family in this period involves listening in a desire to support but also to find a 'key' for preaching. The 'key' can be an incident or words spoken by or shared with the deceased, a favourite Bible verse in his/her life. It is often something the mourners are familiar with or something they would like to know about the deceased.[182] This can be an arresting way of holding the attention of the congregation as the biblical text is shared. I have struggled for such a key often but on other occasions the 'key' came unexpectedly. This happened to me recently.

My aunt died unexpectedly in 2016 and I was to preach in her funeral. It would not be easy, for she was close to my mother, my brother and myself. However, I found a key. Let me explain. Several months previously, my brother had been critically ill after major surgery. On my first visit to him, he was unconscious in a Critical Care Unit and the staff instructed family to keep talking to him though he was unconscious. I related family news to him, then a sermon I had just preached on 1 John 4:10. Later that day I drove some distance to share news of my brother with my aunt. It was a precious time. I repeated what I had shared in the hospital. Her probing questions helped me apply the text for her. In her funeral I preached on 1 John 4:10 to an unchurched congregation, explaining the association of the Bible text with my aunt. It was a 'key' enabling me to hold their attention while declaring the gospel. For the congregation, the gospel was accessible. However, the preacher may fail to find a key, so that is another reason for spending time with mourners prior to the funeral, highlighting the importance of the pastor being relational and developing inter-personal skills, despite shyness and feelings of inferiority.

Accountable

The Bible underlines the accountability of ministers/elders to God for the quality and faithfulness of their work. Ezekiel was warned if he failed to deliver God's Word as commanded then their 'blood I will require at your hand' (Ezek. 3:17-19). Patrick Fairbairn, commenting on these words, emphasised that the ministry of the Word on all occasions should be 'plied with unwearied diligence, with affectionate tenderness and fervency of spirit; for the work is of infinite importance, and results past reckoning depend on it.'[183] Another example is the apostle Paul addressing the Ephesus church elders (Acts 20:20, 26; Heb. 13:17).

A major challenge is referring to hell and the wrath of God. The Lord's own handling of the subject in His ministry is helpful. Most of the direct references to hell in the New Testament came from His lips and are located predominantly in the Synoptic Gospels. The Lord used the teaching sensitively, depending on the attitude of His congregation. He did not preach hell indiscriminately. Nor must we. Rather He used the doctrine sparingly but only after people had been under His teaching for some time and hardened their hearts to His message. His use of this teaching was purposeful, related to the attitude of His audience as illustrated in Matthew 8:12, Mark 9:43-48 and Luke 16:19-31.

How does this relate to funeral preaching? If we are preaching the meta-narrative of the gospel 'drama', the warning element will be implicit in pressing the urgent need to be reconciled to God. This doctrine of wrath is integral to the 'drama' of God's unique saving action in Christ, but this must be declared with compassion and discretion. Those sitting under the Word in the funeral service are 'the future dead', so the drama of Christ's decisive victory over sin, death, hell and Satan must be emphasised. One thing is clear. The gospel's meta-narrative is urgently needed in our society.

3.   DISCIPLINE

The preacher needs to exercise discipline with regards to the length, language, love and liveliness of his preaching in funerals—normally a vast majority of mourners are unchurched. These points are now fleshed out.

Length

Sometimes discipline is imposed upon ministers in a cremation service where the available time is restricted. A brief message must be aimed for. If the service is held in a church building, there is more flexibility.

On two occasions, I was unnecessarily long which I regret, for it was an additional strain on mourners. There is no virtue in being long!

Language

Increasingly, a funeral service will be attended by a majority of unchurched people biblically illiterate. Key Bible words should be simply explained for people to understand. One term needing explanation now is 'sin', which is not confined to murderers, rapists or child abusers but assumes its significance in relation to God. Likewise, the 'blood' of Christ must be explained in terms of the Lord's death in bearing our sin—the unchurched do not make that connection. Again, 'faith' is not what is commonly understood as general belief or hope that things may improve but rather includes a basic knowledge of the gospel, personal awareness of sin/guilt and the need to be reconciled to God. But the vital aspect of faith has the Lord Jesus Christ, crucified and risen, as its object. It is to Christ personally and directly we go and in Him we trust. We must review the language employed in preaching by explaining key terms simply and faithfully.

Love

Professionalism creeps into the ministry in subtle ways, even in funerals. What the public sometimes experience is a clergyman leading the service and committal in a detached manner. They may refer to a 'cold' service which 'did not do anything for us'. For some clergy, the motive in taking the funeral is financial rather than compassion; it can be a lucrative sideline! John Piper ends one chapter by praying about this danger of professionalism: 'Banish professionalism from our midst, Oh God, and in its place put passionate prayer, poverty of spirit, hunger for God, rigorous study of holy things, white-hot devotion to Jesus Christ, utter indifference to all material gain, and unremitting labour to rescue the perishing, perfect the saints, and glorify our sovereign Lord'.[184]

Liveliness

Liveliness in relation to preaching is not essentially gesticulating continually or moving around, shouting or being dramatic. Imagine my surprise one Saturday before preaching in a church centenary service when the pastor gave a brief message during which he walked around, jumped, shouted, then lay on the floor quietly for several seconds to the surprise of the congregation. It was drama of the worst kind as he drew attention to himself. Positively, the preacher's personality must be involved in preaching yet not dominate and thereby detract from the message.

One must go further. The whole person should be involved in preaching rather than stand motionless or speak in a monotonous tone. Rather he should be natural but vary his voice because his heart is gripped by the message and burning with love for Christ and the people. This is the 'liveliness' which ought to characterise our preaching, even in funerals, so that it is not 'dull', 'boring', 'tedious' or 'detached'.

While convalescing after illness, Dr D. Martyn Lloyd-Jones attended a local church where the preacher was commencing a series of sermons from the book of

Jeremiah. The text that day described the pressure Jeremiah felt to preach because God's Word was like a fire in his bones. Lloyd-Jones records he left the service feeling 'I had witnessed something quite extraordinary… the good man was talking about fire as if he were sitting on an iceberg.' It was 'detached', 'cold' and he was 'a living denial of the very thing that he was saying…. There was no enthusiasm, no apparent concern for the congregation.'[185]

If we approach preaching as a drama and also a disciplined, lively declaration then our hearers are more likely to benefit. If we endeavour to approximate to such standards as preachers we will be 'stretched', but in our weakness the Lord will equip us.

One final observation is necessary. Allen Verhey exhorted: 'Let this, however, always be the last word at a funeral, that God has won and will win the victory over death'. He continues: 'Death will be there, of course, and its power will be obvious enough. Death needs no words to tell those gathered, "I have won again. I win every time. I make a mockery of everybody. I destroy every loving relationship. I dash every hope. You, too, all of you, are mine!" But against that shouting silence of death, the Christian funeral has the opportunity and the responsibility to say, "The Lord is risen! The last word belongs to God."'[186]. Professor Robert Letham,[187] in a personal email to the author,[188] declares: 'I agree that the test of a preacher is preaching at a funeral—it's operating on the edge of life and death, heaven and hell… and the difference between a Christian funeral and the rest is absolutely stark. If a preacher cannot seize that opportunity, he should not be in the pulpit'.

In the next chapter we will consider, pastorally, the complex subject of grief.

7

GRIEF: A PASTORAL PERSPECTIVE

My training for the Christian ministry was almost wholly academic and I felt this lack when assuming my first pastoral charge. As a pastor, having a few godly pastors in my region with whom I could fellowship was encouraging, as was the annual pastors conference in 'Bala'—an oasis for pastors, providing teaching, fellowship and prayer.[189] Pastoral theology remains at the heart of this conference, so one returned encouraged to serve the church. I confess though that I learnt more about pastoral care in the ministry itself, though in the early years it was a sharp learning curve. Grief was something I wrestled with as a pastor, and in a large pastorate I found I was regularly ministering to families with profound grief and sadness over the death of close relatives and friends. Occasionally the circumstances were tragic. In this chapter I attempt to basically describe what grief is and how we can respond.

GRIEF: UNDERSTANDING

His grief was overwhelming and C. S. Lewis describes it vividly in his book, *A Grief Observed*.[190] He married Joy Davidman in 1956 after spending years as a bachelor. His bride was an American poet who already had two young children; the marriage was an extremely happy one. Lewis felt fulfilled, but tragedy struck. After only four years of blissful marriage, his wife died of cancer. It was a huge disappointment. His new world of joy collapsed; in its place came darkness and loneliness.

The book is based on notes written by himself over the months following his wife's death in which he described his grief. His struggles with grief and probing of God's providence in the suffering and death of his wife are striking. He bares open his heart, describing his grief movingly and in ways we can identify with. For Lewis, grief included 'fear... or perhaps more like suspense', 'restlessness', feeling 'mildly drunk or concussed' and 'dreading moments when the house is empty'. Grief also involved 'tears and pathos'.[191] But there is more. 'No one ever told me about the laziness of grief... I loathe the slightest effort... what does it matter now?' His wife's children were embarrassed when he talked about her, as were his friends and colleagues. Lewis also explains 'my heart and body are crying out, come back, come back... I can't settle down. I yawn, I fidget'. In fact, 'I am thinking about her nearly always... real words, looks, laughs, and actions of hers'. There were 'feelings, and feelings, and feelings' which overwhelmed him.

Eventually he detected a small ray of light in the darkness of his grief and depression. He reports: 'Something quite unexpected has happened. It came this morning early. For various reasons... my heart was lighter than it had been for many weeks.'[192] The reasons for this were 'various' but not 'mysterious'. For example, he was recovering from 'mere exhaustion', and had indulged in more physical activity the previous day so slept soundly afterwards. That made a difference. And the weather improved, so instead of clouds and mist outside the sun was shining. But he asks: 'Why has no one told me these things'[193] as practical ways of trying to cope with grief? He also began to think positively about God's providence. Was Lewis 'getting over' his grief 'so soon?' He found the question ambiguous—for 'there will be hardly any moment when he forgets it... His whole way of life will be changed... I am learning to get about on crutches... still, there's no denying that in some sense I feel better.' However, this was accompanied by a sense of 'shame... an obligation to prolong one's unhappiness'. He found grief to be a 'process' rather than a 'state', or rather 'like a long valley'.[194]

I have included this detailed description of Lewis's grief for three reasons. One reason is to encourage you to read the book, for his description of grief accurately reflects what many experience. A second reason for including this reference to Lewis is his openness. Lewis implies that we need to be more open in expressing grief. A third reason for including Lewis' description of grief is to warn that not all experiences of grief are identical, so we ought not compare our own grief with that of someone else, not even Lewis. While Lewis' description of grief is interesting and helpful, it relates to his own experience and may not reflect in all aspects what others experience. A final reason for referring to Lewis is that it provides a platform for identifying different models of grief we need to be aware of without imposing one model exclusively upon an individual's experience of grief.

'The Abyss'

Another and contrasting example of grief may be helpful. 'Confronting the abyss: the relationship between bereavement and faith' is the title of a chapter in which the author, Anthony Gardiner, describes part of his personal pilgrimage which has 'been both hard and bitter'.[195] For him, it is 'the journey of grief'—because of the death of his 'wife of eighteen months, a young woman on the verge of motherhood'. The pain of grief seemed 'unbearable' and the 'sense of loss is devastating'. It is like 'an amputation, the tearing away of part of oneself, leaving you maimed, crippled, stumbling—and empty... and the loss is absolute.' Gardiner continues: 'Death robs us of those we love... it can also destroy our world... the experience of ultimate bereavement, the destruction by death of a close, deep and crucial relationship, can seem to strike a deadly blow against the very idea that human existence has meaning... the shattering of that knocks away one of the foundation pillars on which our world stands, and we are left all at sea... We find ourselves standing at the edge of a precipice.'

Trauma

But Anthony Gardiner is a pastor. 'I have shared', he writes, 'with parents the trauma of miscarriage, stillbirth, neonatal death, a fatal accident to a child, the death of the young in many forms'. His own experience was 'not vastly dissimilar', but in sharing grief with parents, he testifies that 'I have also shared something of their journey back from grief, back from the abyss to something like solid ground'. What is this 'solid ground'? Gardiner refers to Jesus and His 'violent killing, human agony and humiliation... Jesus hangs upon the gibbet, alone between earth and heaven. And that terrible cry of desolation: 'My God, my God, why have you abandoned me? He hangs there to the bitter end… Does anyone care?'

From the midst of our grief and pain and loss, we look for someone who will be with us, someone who will simply 'be there'—even in the depths of the abyss, expressing love. In Christ, the 'man of sorrows', acquainted with grief—who is called Immanuel: 'God with us'—I receive the assurance that God is indeed beside us, sharing our suffering; and I learn that the abyss is not an abyss of meaninglessness, but an abyss of love.

I have included the example of Gardiner's grief in order to show the parallels with that of C. S. Lewis, but also the differences. Gardiner also helpfully reminds us of the deep grief of women who suffer miscarriages, still births and the loss of young children from a variety of causes.

Recovery

A national study of bereavement in the United Kingdom in 2015 by the Sue Ryder charity, which provides social care for those at the end of their lives, provided some interesting details.[196] In a study of two thousand people recently bereaved, they found that it is on average a period of two years, one month and four days before those who have lost someone close begin to start 'feeling better'. Men recover more quickly than women. The 'feeling better' stage in the grieving process is when people feel more positive and hopeful, which is evidenced in their coping better with everyday life again. The first year of bereavement is notoriously difficult and painful, especially facing the first Christmas, birthday and anniversaries. Those who were able to share and discuss their grief with someone else often felt better more quickly than others.

The above statistics are interesting but must be treated with caution. With the two powerful examples of Lewis and Gardiner in mind, including the 'solid ground' both discovered, we can consider in more detail the various models of grief.

MODELS OF GRIEF

Familiar terms like grief, mourning and bereavement must be defined. Edith Buglass helps us here.[197] Grief is a personal response to the death of a close relative or friend, expressed emotionally, physically and behaviourally as well as cognitively, socially and spiritually. These were all aspects of C. S. Lewis' grief. Mourning has a narrower application, referring to the visible, outward expression of this grief which may involve crying, panic attacks, restlessness and constant talking about the deceased or visiting a grave. Many features can be involved in this complex, sometimes long, process of mourning. Bereavement is an umbrella term, including grief and mourning, which normally commences from the time of the relative's death. We will confine our attention to grief and sample some major models to understand it.

To prepare us for these models, we need to emphasise that there are different approaches to grief and different classifications. June Hunt offers one approach, distinguishing between 'chronic grief' and 'repressed grief'.[198] The former refers to unresolved, emotional sorrow over a long period in which there is denial. The latter involves the absence of any expressions of grief and perhaps a refusal even to talk about it and carry on living as if nothing had happened.

Hunt proceeds to identify three significant stages in grief. First, the 'crisis stage' which varies in length and intensity—featuring anxiety, fear, sleep loss, confusion, crying, denial, exhaustion and dreams or nightmares. Then there is the 'crucible stage' which can continue for a year or even until death. Sleep loss continues in this stage, accompanied by anger/resentment, bargaining with God, sadness, confusion, denial, depression, guilt, lethargy, loneliness, low self-worth and a longing for the deceased. The final stage Hunt identifies is the 'contentment stage'. Now there slowly emerges a greater interest in and concern for others, appreciation of friends/family, a modified adjustment to purposeful living, greater trust in the Lord and a sense of hope rather than despair concerning the future. Overall a sense of contentment manifests itself.

These three stages for Hunt require 'guidelines' for appropriate grieving. These guidelines include having a genuine but sensitive support system, liberty to cry without shame or guilt, a willingness to engage socially and regularly—shopping, time-out with family and friends or attending church more regularly. Another necessary guideline is to have someone to trust and confide in and with whom at times you can release resentment and anger.[199]

We will recognise many of these details in the models of grief which we will now describe but Hunt's approach illustrates the many attempts being made to understand grief and assist people in responding to it in manageable and realistic ways. But we look at other models of grief now and the various stages they identify.

Stages

A well-known model of grief was introduced by Elisabeth Kubler-Ross in her influential book *On Death and Dying*[200], in 1969. As noted in chapter two, the author represented the Death Awareness Movement—reacting against the 'medicalisation' of death and the 'silence' regarding death. She aimed to encourage people to talk about death and become more aware of it, accepting it as something 'natural' in human life.

In her book, she identified five stages relevant to both dying and grief: denial, anger, bargaining, depression and acceptance. 'Denial' has been described as a 'natural defence system'[201] while 'anger' takes it further in expressing strong feelings as to why one has been bereaved. A person is unwilling to see any reason in it; the 'bargaining' stage can lead on to 'depression' as the stark reality of the situation begins to strike home. A final stage is that of 'acceptance' when a person—whatever the reason—is more at peace within. This model has been developed and increased to seven emotional stages of grief by the addition of shock or disbelief and guilt.

Criticisms of this model are numerous. For example, it is inflexible and too neat, while it is also difficult to ascertain which stage a person has reached. Progression to another stage is also not linear—for stages overlap, often involving several stages at one time, with some people reverting to earlier stages during the process. Consequently, grief is not a static, sequential process. A related criticism is that this model was not built upon empirical data.

Living Around Grief

Persuaded that grief does not disappear or shrink, another model speaks of 'living around grief'. Here grief evolves through four flexible phases which overlap—namely shock, yearning, despair and recovery. More phases ought to be identified but this model is appealing. I have witnessed it in the lives of friends and relatives.

For example, my niece, a Christian, died at the age of fifteen. An attractive, clever teenager who suffered from cystic fibrosis, she enjoyed a close, loving relationship with her mother and brother. I was privileged to share in depth with her. Her lifespan was expected to end in her mid-twenties but she died in hospital unexpectedly while being treated for a chest infection. It was a huge shock for the professionals and family who found it difficult to come to terms with. Her mother's grief did not shrink over the years. The grief was 'always there', even though she carried on with her life and caring for her son. Twenty-seven years later the grief had remained until she died. She carried on with her life yet continued to grieve just as deeply. The difference is that at first her life was consumed by grief but slowly her personal, family, church and social life resurfaced and grew around her grief. There were darker days when she was more deeply aware of grief—weeping often—but even on other days she suffered the same degree of inner grief. What happened is that 'the grief stayed just as big but her life grew around it'.[202] I suspect this is true for many.

Attachment

A further model—'attachment'—also underpins the previous model. Here strong affectional bonds are developed from infancy or over the years. John Bowlby's theory[203] views grief as an instinctive, universal response to separation, so it is a predictable response. C. M. Parkes is in substantial agreement, viewing grieving as a process with a series of responses to the death of a loved one. He refers to an initial shock and possibly a numbness, leading to intense grief, often accompanied by physical symptoms such as stress, chest pain, shortness of breath, loss of appetite and insomnia. A lack of concentration is common too. These symptoms are aggravated when a person seeks to suppress feelings.[204]

The depth of grief is determined by the depth of affection and intimacy enjoyed by the mourner with the person who died. C. S. Lewis is an example of an intense, intimate and affectional bond with his wife over four years. For others, the bond extends over a longer period.

Unique

One more model underlines the 'uniqueness' of each individual. The term phenomenology is used in psychology/psychotherapy to explain how each person will experience and respond differently to a similar event. This approach majors on the individual's subjective experience, focusing upon his or her perceptions and feelings. In this way, one can move towards understanding how each person will experience and respond differently to a similar event. No one model is imposed on the person's experience. Often the family dynamic is extremely important in understanding grief, as well as the intimacy and length of the relationship with the deceased. Here is a recent example of this model I am very familiar with.

A friend's mother died yet she was unable to cry or grieve. While the friend is a warm and caring person, her mother was cold, selfish and unloving towards her; she never expressed love in any way, not even embracing or putting her to bed as a child. Not one kiss was ever given to the daughter. The grandparents lived with them so she was left in their care from the earliest years and the mother socialised. While the grandparents loved her, our friend still longed for a mother's affection. Her response consequently to her mother's death has been complex—governed by their poor, distant relationship for over fifty years, with all the emotions, hurt and rejection experienced.

Each individual is unique so no one model will provide a universal framework for counselling. Ann Dent acknowledges that 'each person is unique and will deal with a significant death in their own way; therefore there is no one right or wrong way to grieve.'[205]

Other factors contribute to the uniqueness of our individual experiences of the same event. Apart from our background and family relationships, personality and temperament—together with beliefs—also contribute to the mix of our unique, personal experience of grief. Variations are therefore inevitable, even proper, and that is why we need wisdom and flexibility but also patience and love in comforting and pastoring those in grief.

Summary

Our sample of models indicates some features which overlap. A look at John 11 shows us how the Lord Himself responded to the death of someone He loved. The response of the Lord Jesus to the death of His close friend Lazurus is deeply instructive and challenging for us.

There was a divine, purposeful delay in the Lord's visit to the home of Lazarus to comfort his sisters, Mary and Martha. Lazarus had been dead and lying in the cave for four days (John 11:17). The first official three days of mourning were now over and decomposition of the body had set in. Hearing that Jesus was approaching their home, Martha rushed out to meet Him and before long she heard those memorable words of Jesus: 'I am the resurrection and the life' (v. 25). These words of Christ need to be uppermost in our thoughts in fellowshipping with those who grieve. We also draw attention to the response of the Lord: 'he groaned (deeply moved) in the spirit and was troubled'(v. 33). He felt agony in these sad circumstances and burst into tears (v. 35)—but these were genuine tears in which He felt the anguish and sorrow of the mourners. His own heart identified with them.

But there is so much more as well. The Lord's response and feelings in verses 33 and 38 express His agitation and outburst of grief. D.A. Carson suggests 'he was outraged in spirit'[206] while B. B. Warfield refers to His 'inexpressible anger'[207] in approaching the grave of Lazarus. No doubt He was angry with the hypocrisy of the professional mourners who grieved insincerely like pagans for the required three days. The uncontrolled grief and despair of the sisters was possibly a factor but more likely His indignation is directed towards the presence of death in God's world. His heart was full of compassion and concern but in the big picture He had come into the world to deliver people from sin and the cruel bondage of death. He achieved this in His death and resurrection, then in the eventual glorification of the church. He approached the grave of Lazarus and death as a mighty soldier to confront the ugly power of death—but He was assured of victory. Here is a picture of what He would achieve days later in Jerusalem.

This narrative is extremely instructive in understanding the Lord's approach to the death of a loved one. Before leaving John 11, there is the challenge for us all in facing death and grief to see and believe the big picture of the Lord's triumph over sin, death, hell and the devil. The bereaved need to recognise and engage with their grief in meaningful ways but it is essential for feelings of grief to be expressed rather than suppressed. Paradoxically, while grief should be expressed, it can become excessive and unwise for a variety of reasons, so appropriate control is necessary as the individual is encouraged to adjust to the new situation and rebuild their lives around the grief. In counselling, there is need to be flexible, open-minded, non-judgmental and never shocked on hearing expressions of grief. Nor should we be in a hurry to impose our own interpretation of grief upon the individual, or allow our personal experience of grief to dominate our counselling. Each individual response to grief is different and must be respected.

Listening is crucial—some church visitors, even relatives, talk too much, often unhelpfully. There is wisdom in the friends of Job who silently sat by him in his affliction for days. And when they spoke, they showed they had misinterpreted the purpose of the trials which Job had experienced. Visiting and being alongside the individual/family at strategic times of need is often necessary, yet we must allow for the fact that the process of grief is untidy and may not follow expected stages. Some individuals, as we have seen, move around their emotions of grief deliberately but non-sequentially and may even have a preference for some aspects of the grief then remain there. There is need for flexibility, compassion and careful listening—wisely avoid over-reliance on a pastor/counsellor.

Following the instruction of the apostle Paul in 1 Thessalonians 4:18 and 5:11 we must 'comfort one another with these words' of a glorious future in heaven and eventual glorification when the Lord returns. Be sensitive to the situation. Perhaps the person being visited is extremely tired or not ready to talk, or there may be family members waiting to spend time with that person. Do not talk—certainly not excessively—about your own grief or illness. A surprising number of people do this and fail to give proper attention to the one they are visiting. The visit is not about you. Maximise on reading the Word of God if possible, then praying. This may need to be brief or you may have to be content with referring to a Bible verse/s as you converse. Informal visits over a longer period to the grieving person can be encouraging as s/he adjusts to life without their relative. Grief does not end when the funeral is over. The most important role you have in caring is to pray faithfully for them and for the Lord to give them grace, peace and reality in believing.

We turn in the next chapter to consider pastoral care in churches.

8
Pastoral Care in Churches

Some churches exercise genuine pastoral care and counselling, expressing the love of God practically. They long to do more. Other churches are deficient in such care—for a variety of reasons. One significant factor in the United Kingdom is the number of small church congregations which are elderly, discouraged and leaderless, although there is considerable potential for growth in their communities. This is a matter for urgent prayer and consideration by Christians. This chapter aims to foster pastoral care in churches in several related ways—by first discussing leadership, then raising practical questions.

Church officers are key to pastoral care and that is why I begin with them; their character, spirituality, and example in caring for people are crucial for the church. To lack suitably gifted leaders in any church, however small, is serious. In focusing on pastoral care in general at this point, rather than on leaderless churches or majoring on caring for the sick, dying and bereaved, there are four reasons for this strategy. Firstly, along with church officers, the members determine the quality and extent of pastoral care within the church—with a ripple effect on the dying and bereaved. Rather than dealing superficially with poor pastoral care, we are attempting to address the major causes of the problem. That is not easy but this is where we begin. Secondly, church officers need to recognise that their teaching and example or lack of it has an impact on the church, including pastoral care. Thirdly, if individuals and families in the church are cared for pastorally and loved consistently over a long or a brief period of time, this will be a support when they face difficulties, illness or bereavement. Some churches only switch on their 'pastoral care' hat when individuals are in crisis, then remove the hat fairly quickly afterwards! Pastoral care must be on-going and comprehensive. Care for the dying and the grieving is only one area of the whole church reaching out in love and prayer to one another, irrespective of their needs or circumstances. There is a fourth reason for our focus. Recognising the needs of small and elderly gospel churches, one can encourage other churches blessed with gifted leaders to assist such needy churches. This is happening—with encouraging examples of a larger church commissioning a few members with an elder to settle in a small fellowship. In some situations, after a brief period, a pastor is called and the church grows.

By developing good leadership in churches and fostering pastoral care, it is hoped that churches can also support a weaker, needy church in their area. These are reasons why our focus is now being subsumed under the general subject of pastoral care.

Leadership

Local church pastoral care is normally expressed through pastors/elders, deacons and members. There are many variations depending on church polity, the numerical strength, age range, gifts of members, and location. The term 'church leaders', rarely used in the Bible, is shorthand for those holding church office.[208] The term has secular connotations and, while we can learn from them, churches should not be dominated by secular models. Here I attempt a more radical reappraisal of biblical data regarding church officers as a basis for what follows.

There are often tensions between church officers and members—so there is an urgent need for officers to be more self-critical and accountable, even with regard to expressing and fostering effective pastoral care. Donald M. Macdonald emphasises the following aspects of church leaders: 'leadership is theological, ecclesial and evangelical. Desire for the glory of God, the welfare of the church and the advance of the gospel must shape the form of leadership... Church leaders must be godly in character; they must have a thorough understanding of the church and a pastor's heart; and they must love the gospel of Christ and long to see others come to know him. Furthermore, leadership is never to be invested in a single individual'.[209] We can now fill in some of these essential features of church leaders.

Character: Biblical Reasons

A holy, Christlike character tops the list biblically in prioritising the qualities required for church leadership (1 Tim. 3 and Titus 1). This is important in our contemporary amoral and 'post-truth' situation and dare not be compromised, even in a small church desperate to appoint a 'leader'. Consider the biblical demand for holiness, as Sinclair Ferguson so helpfully summarises it from the apostle Peter's epistle: 'God the Holy Trinity is devoted to it. God the Holy Father has commanded us to pursue it. Christ the Holy Son has died to effect it. The Holy Spirit works in us to bring forth the fruit of it. God sends trials into our experience in order to produce it. Heaven itself is a place that is full of it.'[210] The entire redemptive purpose of God calls, and cries out, for the holiness of all believers. Holiness is not an option for any church officer or believer.

1. CHARACTER: BIBLICAL QUALIFICATIONS FOR CHURCH OFFICERS

Unsurprisingly, qualifications for church elders/pastors/deacons in 1 Timothy 3 and Titus 1 emphasise holy character. Notice briefly the requirements. They must be beyond reproach, show fidelity if married, leading their families lovingly and biblically. A good reputation inside and outside the church is also required. 'Self-control' is compulsory, especially in avoiding bouts of temper, impatience, a critical spirit or greediness. A 'controlling' approach to people, the use of violence and unguarded speech disqualifies men from office. In addition, spiritual maturity and the gift to teach are necessary, but the teaching gift is dwarfed by the heavy emphasis on moral character.

Moral requirements dare not be compromised but to what extent are they expected and cultivated in churches?

Character: A Contrast to False Teachers

The Bible indicates that false teaching undermines holy behaviour. Reminiscent of the Lord's teaching (Matt. 7:15-

27), the apostles warn concerning ungodly, immoral behaviour, resulting from error. In 1 Thessalonians 2:1-12, Paul contrasts his own godly ministry with that of false teachers (1 Tim. 6:3-11), whereas Peter identifies the characteristics of false teachers, drawing attention to their 'destructive ways' (2 Pet. 2:1-3). Lax morals preached, practiced and encouraged by these heretics contradicted Christ's holy gospel. False teaching often results in unholy living. On the other hand, inconsistent behaviour on the part of men who preach the Word faithfully dishonours the Lord, bringing the church and the gospel into disrepute.

Character: Our Contemporary Situation Demands it
In one trip to Korea, a taxi driver drove me to a preaching appointment. I asked if he was a Christian. He informed me he was a Buddhist but had many Christian friends. I was intrigued. 'Why are you not a Christian?' He replied: 'I do not want to be a 'Sunday Christian' like my friends. One day I will become 'a real Christian' and live like a Christian should'.

He had identified a major weakness in many churches worldwide. In our amoral society, increasing numbers of moral failures are occurring amongst professing Christians but there is no substitute for holy living, not even orthodox preaching!

2.   CHARACTER: PASTORAL CARE DEMANDS IT

Like all Christians, church officers are sinners who easily backslide, fall into sin or can be misled by false teaching. That is a red light to be taken seriously so these men can also be exposed in pastoral care situations. Because of the wide mix of complex pastoral challenges confronting churches, like marriage/divorce, conflict, pornography, child abuse, domestic abuse, integrity, backsliding, grief, or even concerns about Christian assurance and experience— godly character is essential when pastoring in these intimate situations.

Again, do motives like financial gain, popularity, control, or even physical attraction tempt us? Are graces like godliness, integrity, transparency, trustworthiness, prayerfulness and an ardently genuine love for the Lord and His people evident in our lives? Congregations are crying out to be cared for by such people. Are our homes and relationships permeated by love and harmony or by anger, impatience, temper and abuse? Or are we amongst the nearly 70 per cent of internet users visiting porn sites secretly? We must be 'taking heed' to ourselves (1 Tim. 4:16, Acts 20:28).

Care is necessary too when counselling women. In the light of Titus 2:3-5, older godly women should be freed to teach and care for younger women as well as their peers. Here is an important ministry and in some churches a godly gifted woman is appointed to work pastorally amongst women, relieving and protecting male officers. This can work well.

Kevin DeYoung's book, *The Hole In Our Holiness*, challenges our lax attitudes to holy living. He observes: 'There is a gap between our love for the gospel and our love for godliness. This must change. It's not pietism, legalism, or fundamentalism to take holiness seriously. It's the way of all those who have been called to a holy calling by a holy God.'[211] He then describes what holiness looks like in everyday life: 'holiness looks like the renewal of God's image in us' and it 'looks like a life marked by virtue instead of vice'. Holiness also 'looks like a clean conscience' and 'like obedience to God's commands', but finally, it 'looks like Christlikeness'.[212]

This is what God desires for all His people and that example of holy living must be provided by church officers. We turn in the next section to consider three practical questions.

QUESTIONS

I am frequently asked questions about pastoral care so I share three of the more common questions for your reflection—and I offer them for discussion and prayer by churches.

Q1: 'Should a pastor major exclusively on preaching and prayer rather than visiting? Or should he visit and give himself to the Word and prayer?'

There is confusion concerning the answer and the biblical principles are debated and variously interpreted and applied, but it is a controversial question which keeps resurfacing in churches—sometimes in the context of grievances and misunderstandings. Different answers are given with some answers unsettling, even disappointing, congregations.

On one side, it is argued that visiting can reduce the time available for adequate sermon preparation, reading and prayer. The latter is the pastor's primary task (Acts 6:3-4). Combining both visiting, counselling and preparation for preaching with prayer can lead to frustration for the pastor and even the congregation, but for different reasons. Again, it is unrealistic to expect one person like the pastor to shoulder all the responsibility for visiting in addition to public ministry. It is not a one-man ministry which the church exercises. Another factor is that if pastors visit often they may indirectly discourage members from serving in their biblical role of caring for one another. Furthermore, too much visiting in addition to a demanding public ministry can lead to pastoral burn-out, affecting the quality of preaching/teaching. This is not easily or always recognised. Finally, if church elders are functioning biblically then they are shouldering the work of pastoral care alongside the pastor and relieving him so he can give himself to more prayer and preparation for preaching.

These arguments need to be wrestled with biblically and realistically in the light of the church's needs and those of the pastor. Not all pastors can handle the same volume of work or pressure—so comparing pastors and their capacity for work is unhelpful. Pastors vary considerably in personality, temperament, gifts, training and capacity for work. Some men are not multi-taskers while others take much longer to prepare messages.

From a different perspective, some suggest that the preceding arguments are overstated. The question does not necessarily demand an either-or answer. If an appropriate balance is maintained by the pastor in prioritising prayer and the ministry of the Word and with elders sharing pastoral work, then the pastor can also be involved in appropriate visiting and counselling. Remember too that the example of care for the congregation by both pastor and elders can stimulate members themselves to express the same care for each other.

From experience, a pastor's visiting and availability for the sick, dying, grieving and other needy individuals/ families can enrich one's praying and sermon preparation rather than detract from it. Their questions, concerns and struggles influence preaching positively in terms of themes and biblical passages chosen and application—so the Word is communicated more relevantly. Furthermore, the preacher develops in this way a closer relationship with the people, and perhaps they will listen more eagerly to the preacher!

It is important to consider this question in depth and agree with the pastor or a future pastor, elders and congregation, in order to avoid potential difficulties but more importantly to encourage openness and mutual respect with a view to ensuring adequate and loving pastoral care for all the church. This is a key area for reflection and prayer.

Q2: 'Should a church carefully plan its ministry of care and visiting?'

In some churches, the pastor does nearly all the visiting so little organisation is required, perhaps because there is a small, elderly and dependent congregation. This model may be imposed on the church due to the age and limitations of members or even the pastor's preference. That is a model being played out in numerous churches across the United Kingdom. A significant number of these churches may close within ten or fifteen years. Although the pastor is gifted and his visits appreciated, the model is flawed—because when the pastor leaves or is ill or on holiday then pastoral care stops.

By contrast, other churches may use one of the three following models.

The first model is where visiting is led by the pastor who encourages a few members to help, possibly alongside another church officer. This is left to the pastor's personal discretion in enlisting help. The model is pastor-dependent but has the advantages of spontaneity and little organisation. Negatively, it often fails to encourage the whole church to engage in mutual care.

Another model is where the pastor/elders involve members more formally in the visiting team. Care is usually taken in identifying godly women and men, often those who are older and can be trusted in visiting the sick and grieving. In my local church this system works well, with one person giving names of individuals or couples needing visits. In some meetings of the church, including the monthly communion service, individuals who are ill or bereaved will be mentioned to the church for prayer and even visiting, where appropriate. This is a more organized approach and ladies often visit in groups of twos. However, the pastor also visits, as do the elders, and some deacons— depending on circumstances. In the regular elders' sessions, pastoral needs are shared before spending time in prayer for the church. I prefer this model—for it is organised but flexible, effective and encourages other believers in the church to care for one another. Currently a growing number of members are spontaneously visiting others in the church who are ill or in need.

The third model is more organised. For example, a church in England has two teams. One is the KITES team (Keeping In Touch with Elderly Sick), providing regular visitation of the elderly and sick and the Bereavement Team. In the latter, there are two female leaders with a total of seven in the team, including an elder. The majority have followed a counselling course or have experience in counselling. The church paid for three team members to go on a Cruse Counselling course which they found valuable and recommended pastors go on it!

As soon as they hear of a bereavement, the entire team is informed, as well as the elders. A card and flowers are sent, then one or more of the team visit the bereaved. At least one of them attends the funeral and a record is kept of those who have died with the aim of remembering the anniversary of the death. There is close liaison with pastor/elders, yet they acknowledge it is not a perfect system and improvements are regularly made. They regard this model as being better than one person having sole responsibility for the sick and grieving in the church.

But is it too organised? Does it fail to involve more of the church in pastoral care? On at least two of the models described, more people in the church are involved in the ministry of care. That is right because of the priesthood of all believers and also because of the church's corporate unity with the need to encourage mutual care.

Q3: 'Are there helpful examples of pastoral care we can learn from?'

There are many historical as well as contemporary churches and individuals worldwide which provided or continue to provide good pastoral care. I resist the temptation to use historical examples and will only refer to one recent example because it ticks many boxes which are important. Here are the details.

Won Sang Lee is the most humble and prayerful pastor I have met; it is a huge claim to make, especially after meeting so many godly pastors over the years. I met this Korean-American pastor ten years ago when he was eager to pursue PhD studies and I was appointed as his research supervisor. His research sought to evaluate his twenty-six years ministry in the same Presbyterian church in the United States. He had two aims. One was to assess critically his own ministry, a task notoriously difficult to achieve. His ministry had been evaluated externally 1999-2000, with the findings published in 2005.[213] This evaluation was undertaken by author, Thom S. Rainer, and a competent research team. Lee's church was eventually chosen as one of thirteen out of 52,333 potential American churches which met strict criteria. These criteria required the church to be evangelistic, having had a minimum of twenty-six conversions in the previous five years, provide evidence of decline in attendance in past years followed by sustained growth of at least five years—a growth which was continuing. Finally, all the criteria must have been met during the same pastor's leadership! Others too were aware of the significant growth and influence of his church in a Virginia suburb of Washington, DC—in close proximity to the White House.[214] Won Sang Lee approached his research by identifying major principles controlling his ministry.

That was his first aim but a second aim was to enter into conversation across the centuries with John Chrysostom (347-407 A.D.), in an attempt to identify pastoral principles undergirding his ministry. Chrysostom was chosen because Rev. Lee greatly respected his writings on leadership, with its emphasis on spirituality, integrity, compassion, preaching and caring for the people. Chrysostom was from Syria where his godly mother nurtured him in the Christian faith; she claimed God had called her to devote her time and energies to this task. Baptised at the age of twenty, he devoted himself to serving Christ. Following his mother's death, he withdrew for four years to develop self-discipline—studying the Bible night and day. Ordained in 386, he served in Antioch until 397 as preacher and pastor, ministering with 'great passion and uncompromising integrity'[215], as well as compassion. Later, hearing reports of his preaching and pastoral oversight, the Emperor influenced the bishops to install him as the pastor of Constantinople, partly because of religious corruption there. Here, Chrysostom faced extensive opposition and this led eventually to his premature death in 407. Dr Lee's second aim therefore, of entering into conversation with Chrysostom, involved research into his life and writings, including sampling hundreds of his extant sermons/ homilies. Although the situations were vastly different, the research suggested that core principles driving both their ministries were reasonably similar.

The four major principles Won Sang Lee identified in his own ministry were 'caring for people practically but primarily spiritually'; 'the pastor's character of integrity and spirituality'; 'preaching'; and fourthly, 'cross-cultural mission'. Some of the details are challenging. For example, he started his ministry with fourteen families who remained after many church members had left to follow their minister in forming another church nearby due to a bitter division. He prioritised by preaching the Word of God then safeguarding his personal integrity and building congregational trust. Dr Lee began by loving these families who needed encouragement and pastoral care. He visited well, slowly building genuine friendships and mutual trust. 'Paradoxically', he writes, pastoral ministry is 'both people-centred and Christ-centred'[216] with 'shepherding as a key biblical model for pastoral ministry' which 'involves visiting'.

I was also encouraged by his emphasis on the pastor's integrity and spirituality, with the plea for Christlikeness. Humility, he insists, is 'the core feature of integrity'[217], with the Lord Jesus providing this new paradigm of servant leadership throughout his ministry and the paradigm being humility expressed practically in different situations as illustrated in Mark 10:42-45 and John 13:15, but supremely in Philippians 2:5-11. Such humility is also demonstrated in devoting oneself to prayer and increasing dependence on the living God. And this pastor lived it daily, not merely talked about it!

He views preaching as 'the central focus and climax of public worship'; the Word too should be prominent in evangelism. For that reason, when he became aware of the call to preach, he felt his inadequacy and the urgency of obtaining a 'good theological training' coupled with a thorough grasp of the biblical languages in order to expound the Word faithfully.

His fourth principle of cross-cultural mission expressed his passion to obey the Great Commission (Matt. 28:18-20) by pursuing international mission alongside local and national engagement in mission.

I continue to be challenged by his example of pastoral care; that is the reason for choosing this example to answer the question. Dr Wong Sang Lee's example challenges churches to critically review the quality of pastoral care being exercised over the Lord's people. The pastor needs to be a caring, compassionate and Christlike man whose integrity is apparent for all to observe. This will be confirmed in suggesting a pastoral care model from Romans chapter twelve and that will be the theme of the next chapter.

9
Concluding Challenges in Pastoral Care

The pastoral care of people in local churches, including the dying and bereaved, is extremely important. Hopefully that message has been sounded clearly in this book and the theme is continued in this final chapter but from a different perspective.

Challenges

There is no easy or slick answer to the lack of pastoral support in churches and that is why in this chapter we are discussing three practical but basic challenges in an attempt to strengthen pastoral care; in doing so, we will identify some harsh realities in different church situations, including the vulnerability of church leaders themselves. You may wonder whether this is necessary in a book dealing with the subject of dying and grief. My answer to such a query will be brief.

During years of pastoring churches and also training pastors, I have witnessed not only the demise of some churches but also a tendency of church leaders in failing to pastor adequately the people in their care and to be alongside Christians, especially in their deepest needs when dying and grieving. Too often I have heard, and still hear, the anguished cries from some Christians that no one cares for them or takes the trouble to visit and pray with them. I am insisting that not only should church leaders be biblically and theologically informed but, in addition, their godliness and deep relationship to the Lord needs to be expressed genuinely in caring for people. Even Christians who are informed that they are terminally ill desire and need prayer, fellowship and encouragement in the Word from a pastor or elder. Those grieving too can experience considerable darkness, emptiness and profound loss so they value support and love. Such examples can be multiplied, but I fear that often church officers can be ill-equipped in holiness, prayer , an intimate knowledge of the Lord and a heart love for the people. This is an observation rather than a criticism; it is an appeal, not a negative dismissal of the good work being done. That is why in this final chapter we are attempting to address three harsh but basic realities which affect pastoral care in different ways. The first reality and challenge is a logistical one .

1. LOGISTICAL CHALLENGES

With the alarming decline in church attendance and membership in many parts of the United Kingdom, some churches face logistical challenges—with only a few members and a lack of leadership. A major consequence is that there may be no one available to care for those with a terminal illness or suffering bereavement. I know friends where there is no one to pray and encourage them in the

Word, a situation which prevails especially in rural areas of the United Kingdom. In addressing this challenge, I am seeking to convey their desperate plea for help and prayer. The logistical difficulties facing small, struggling churches need to be recognised by us and shared for prayer. Allow me, however, to provide a wider and contrasting picture from my own pastoral experience.

In the two churches I pastored I had to shoulder the major responsibility for pastoral care. In the first pastorate, despite a large membership and twelve church elders, the tradition was for the pastor to shoulder mostly all the pastoral work and visiting. Even if an elder visited an individual/family the pastor was still expected to visit. My second pastorate was a bilingual church plant and I was the first pastor. There was a small membership of fourteen and on Sundays the members went either to the English or Welsh language services. As it was a university city, there were many students attending the Sunday services as well as professional workers, academics and local people. Logistically the situation approximated more to a preaching station than a local church. Many people, however, wanted the pastor's help. I was stretched and even holiday visitors during the summer often needed pastoral advice and encouragements, including pastors. It was difficult coping logistically with the varied pastoral demands. By contrast, currently I am an elder in a church with a congregation of four hundred people in Sunday services with a good range of ages, young families as well as young people. Many attend the church prayer meeting, too. In addition to a pastor and elders, there are two full-time staff workers—including a womens' worker—plus several deacons, so the church is blessed. The church provides extensive pastoral care with a significant number of members also involved spontaneously in caring for people in the congregation.

I recognise this is not the norm for many churches. You are entitled to ask the inevitable question: how can anyone in such a privileged church situation appreciate the problems facing smaller, struggling churches in providing pastoral care? My answer is three-fold. First of all, in my first pastoral charge, Presbytery insisted that one Sunday each month ministers should preach in a pastorless church, administer Holy Communion and encourage members. On these Sundays, the congregations were small and elderly, often the elders were either elderly and/or restricted by ill-health from exercising pastoral care. I met or heard of members on such visits who were dying or bereaved but no one was available locally to support them pastorally. It was heart-breaking. Sometimes I was able to visit them or share with them after a church service but they needed frequent support. Monthly we faced such situations and tragically nearly all these small village churches have since closed. Could I have done more? Yes. Should the Presbytery have been more visionary and pro-active? Yes, undoubtedly. There was the opportunity to be visionary, but the shortage of ordained ministers, limited financial resources and a growing number of pastorless churches within Presbytery made it extremely difficult to help on a meaningful basis. However, I lament the fact we did not do more to help those churches maintain a witness in their communities.

The situation in the United Kingdom has continued to deteriorate with local churches of different denominations struggling to continue, with many having closed or are about to close their doors permanently. Who will care for these scattered believers, especially those with desperate spiritual and physical needs? The situation is desperate.

Although I disagree with the claim, one national newspaper recognised the serious plight of churches nationwide and predicted on the basis of current trends that Christianity in the UK will come to an end in 2067.[218] Against this background, holding regular public preaching services, prayer meetings and exercising pastoral care in some struggling churches will be almost impossible soon and this ought to stir larger churches to assist, where possible.

Encouraging

Secondly, there are encouraging signs. One is that a small number of stronger churches have encouraged a few of their members with leadership potential, some with young children, to join a nearby struggling church with their blessing in order to ensure biblical teaching, pastoral care and evangelism continues there. For some Christians, this was a temporary arrangement for a couple of years, while others settled permanently and are contributing pastorally to the life of a weaker church. This is an encouraging development.

Near London, for example, a struggling Congregational church in a quaint but remote village has been transformed due to the intervention of a large Baptist church, approximately ten miles away. Twelve church members, including an elder and an organist, were encouraged to travel to this small church and identify themselves with that fellowship for as long as necessary. The church was also visionary in appointing a gifted young man to become the pastor although he needed to engage in part-time secular work to provide for his young family. This church is now secured for the foreseeable future and exercises a biblical witness in the village.

INTER-RELATEDNESS

Thirdly and relatedly, while some Protestant denominations and groups are exploring ways of helping weak churches and also planting new churches, a more co-ordinated and vigorous attempt is needed to get alongside weak churches. Presbyterian denominations have their own resources and procedures for assisting weaker churches within their presbyteries.

There are encouragingly helpful examples of this in North East England over the past decade or more and I applaud what has been achieved. It has been visionary. Other examples can be referred to. Within Independency, the picture is patchy, but assistance remains dependent often on the vision of a larger church or group of churches. There are instances of such help being given within the Evangelical Fellowship of Congregational Churches (EFCC) and in the Fellowship of Independent Evangelical Churches (FIEC).

My personal preference is for Presbyterian church polity but having experienced Independency for some years, improvements are needed to express the unity of local churches. Trusting the same Saviour, embracing the supreme authority of God's Word, indwelt by the one Holy Spirit, ruled over by the supreme head of the church, the Lord Jesus Christ while facing the same enemy and engaged in the Great Commission, local churches need each other. And here I appeal for help on behalf of struggling, elderly congregations which will close soon without assistance. Can these tiny, faithful congregations be rescued from oblivion? The clock is ticking, with some tiny fellowships of believers currently lacking pastoral care, so those bereaved or dying amongst them have no pastoral support.

2. PERSONAL CHALLENGES

A second challenge is more personal—for some pastors and church officers struggle in terms of their own personality or lack of experience to lead their church and exercise pastoral care. Some pastors, for example, are happy to preach the Word publicly yet feel out of their depth coping with individuals or families pastorally. They may be weak in inter-personal skills which inhibit them from caring pastorally, as needed by the church.

Here are pastoral challenges which are rarely discussed. Should the dying and bereaved lose out on pastoral support due to the shyness or even invisibility of a pastor or an elder?

SHYNESS

A pastor or elder who cares pastorally for a congregation shoulders an onerous responsibility. Some cope better, while others suffer fatigue and 'burn-out' due to overwork, stress, anxiety and difficult pastoral problems. Sometimes this has a domino effect in weakening the provision of pastoral care. However, there is the less publicised area of natural shyness which inhibits some from caring for people as they and the church would like.

Often colleagues have shared their experiences and struggles over shyness with me and I empathise because I worked my own way through shyness in pastoring churches. The public and social/relational demands upon a pastor in particular can be testing. For example, walking into a crowded room of bereaved relatives is a huge challenge. The situation is tense, yet the pastor feels inadequate and unsure what to say. Or it may be a happier occasion in the church with a buffet and informal fellowship. The pastor is expected to engage with the people socially but he feels like standing alone in a corner or running away.

These are only two of the situations a shy pastor finds difficult to cope with. Can a pastor prevent himself from being paralysed by shyness? There are steps which can help in such situations.

Process

Firstly, overcoming natural shyness is a process rather than a one-off event. It can be a steep learning curve for some over a period of time. It is helpful if a pastor has a trusted elder who initially accompanies him in visiting or advises him in certain situations. Such a supportive friend can exercise a crucial role on this learning curve. Or it may be a wife who encourages and talks her pastor-husband through bouts of shyness and feelings of inadequacy. Such help is invaluable. But it takes time and one should not despair.

Secondly, by trusting the Lord and resting on the promises of God's Word, we can receive courage and grace to cope with demanding situations. We are not on our own. Visiting hospitals, for example, is often demanding in more ways than one. Walking into a large ward, engaging with patients and staff while you are watched and listened to is an uncomfortable experience. On such occasions when fear gripped me, a Bible verse would come forcibly to my mind. I began to realise my foolishness—the Lord would guide and strengthen me; my responsibility was to trust the Lord. These encouraging experiences helped me face similar situations as I learned slowly to challenge my negative responses.

Thirdly, there is the related need to become more self-forgetful. I commend to you Tim Keller's small book, *The Freedom of Self-Forgetfulness*.[219] Many have found its message timely. Keller focuses on 1 Corinthians 3:21-4:7 where Paul shows that the problem underlying divisions in the Corinthian church was pride and boasting; see for example chapter three, verse 21 and chapter four, verse 7. Keller shows from these verses the natural condition of the human ego. In verse six of chapter four, he reminds us that instead of the usual Greek word for pride (*hubris*), the apostle employs *physio* which is only found in the Bible in 1 Corinthians (five times) and once in Colossians. This word for pride literally means overinflated and swollen so this is how Paul describes 'the normal state of the human self'. Christians and church leaders can be 'swollen' and occupied with themselves and their own opinions.

Think of a situation where a person is critical of you. This often happens in a church context or elsewhere. You will probably be offended. By contrast, Paul refers to Christians who are self-forgetful and do not put any value on what people think of them. An ideal? No, for the gospel can transform the human ego. In 1 Corinthians 4:3-4, the apostle says honestly that he does not care what people think of him. Paul's identity and self-worth were independent of what people thought of him or said about him. Keller reminds us of a further significant step the apostle takes. Not only is he unmoved by what people say about him, but he also has a low view of himself. What does he do? He does not indulge in self-hatred in any form but rather boasts in God's acceptance of himself in Christ at great cost. God could not have loved him more or paid a greater price to redeem him. How does this work out practically when we are offended? Keller answers the question: a 'gospel-humble' or 'self-forgetful person would never be hurt particularly badly by criticism'. The reason is that they listen to the criticism and 'see it as an opportunity to change... the more we get to understand the gospel, the more we want to change and be more like Christ. This is gospel-humility, blessed self-forgetfulness. Not thinking more of myself as in modern cultures, or less of myself as in traditional cultures. Simply thinking of myself less.'[220]

Paul looked for an ultimate verdict concerning himself and found it in the gospel—he was justified freely in Christ and lived on the basis of that ultimate verdict. The 'only person whose opinion counts looks at me and finds me more valuable than all the jewels in the earth'. This glorious truth is liberating and encouraging—even for shy people.

Fourthly, one useful piece of advice to a shy pastor is to ask questions on meeting people and to keep on asking questions during the conversation, without giving the impression of conducting an interrogation. The point being that people love talking about themselves, their families, their work or their Christian experience, or their lack of it. This may be a golden opportunity for them to share a personal matter, so pay attention to what they are saying as they may be pastorally needy. By remaining engaged in conversation in this way one is expressing interest in people, their situations or problems, while showing at the same time that they are cared for. In this way people feel they are important and are being listened to. This can be an encouragement so why remain slaves to ourselves? An initial greeting and smile on approaching a person or a group of people followed immediately by a relevant question helps in commencing a conversation, connecting with people and in becoming more self-forgetful and caring.

We turn in the next section to a very different difficulty in pastoral care, namely, how to encourage a church to move forward spiritually. This is a difficulty many pastors face. I have no easy answers, and there is no short-cut, but what I know is that many people in our churches long for quality pastoral support, particularly in meeting the pressing needs of the dying and bereaved. For this reason, I offer two lesser known historical examples before offering biblical principles to guide church leaders in this dilemma.

3. Taking a Church Forward: Historical Encouragement

The third challenge is a more spiritual and corporate one. Even in churches whether small, medium or large, with a pastor and a small team of church officers, there may be frustration and disappointment because the congregation remains complacent and unresponsive to the ministry of the Word; Christians appear indifferent, if not asleep. We are approaching this challenge initially from an historical perspective. Both historical examples relate to North West Wales and the second decade in the nineteenth-century. Despite the space of two hundred years, the principles remain timeless.

Capel-y-Nant

The first example relates to a small Calvinistic Methodist/ Presbyterian church in Capel-y-Nant,[221] located in the delightful area of North West Wales in the Lleyn peninsula—west of the small town of Pwllheli. The church dated back to 1754 with a new building for worship erected in 1782 due to a local revival two years earlier resulting in many conversions and the quickening of believers. For the following thirty-five years the preaching gradually became ineffective and indifference prevailed within the church so one concerned church elder decided to take the initiative and encourage the church, young and old, to memorise Thomas Charles' Catechism.[222] Although the Catechism had 271 questions and answers with a Bible verse, they were brief and memorable statements so through the winter months of 1815-1816 the people memorised the Catechism.

By the summer of 1816, disappointment was felt by the elder as there was still no discernible difference in the church's spiritual life. Fearing that the hard work of preaching and catechising would be wasted, he called the church to pray daily for the preaching and for a period of reviving. In a later meeting, he discovered that all but one had prayed daily so they agreed to continue praying daily for the Lord to prosper the church spiritually. By late December 1816 and January 1817 revival had broken out in the church with many conversions and the enlivening of believers. The church suddenly became fervent in its love and zeal for the Lord.

Beddgelert

This small village, located near the foot of the highest mountain in Wales, Snowdon, is approximately nine miles south of the historical town of Caernarvon on the North Wales coast. Beddgelert had a small Calvinistic Methodist/Presbyterian church with forty members that, like Capel-y-Nant, had known earlier blessing and growth yet now was at a low ebb. The situation was discouraging. Significant social changes were in motion due to the success of the local lead and copper mines which offered good wages and attracted workers from England, Scotland and Ireland. One local resident at the time described the area as 'a terrible, ungodly place', largely because the newly found affluence resulted in drinking, cursing, fighting and immoral behaviour. The four taverns in this ten-mile parish prospered with Beddgelert earning the dubious reputation of being one of the most drunken places in North Wales until 1817. It was consequently an area of spiritual darkness with most of the locals ignorant of the Bible. Only seventeen years earlier a Christian teacher, Robert Jones, had taught in the local school briefly, but the people objected to him teaching the Bible to the younger generation so they openly opposed him. The church itself was discouraged and profoundly disturbed by the changes in the social and moral life of the community and its indifference to the Christian faith. How could the church move forward?

A church elder heard of the blessing in Capel-y-Nant so shared the news with his church in January 1817 but encouraged them to pray daily for the Lord's intervention. Within weeks there were indications of blessing but by August 1817 the Holy Spirit came down in power upon a very ordinary preacher in one of the church's preaching stations[223] with the 'fire' of heaven spreading rapidly through the parish. Days later similar scenes of blessing were experienced in Beddgelert so that by the end of 1817 at least one hundred people had joined the church in profession of faith after being carefully examined and questioned concerning their faith and changed lifestyles. There are principles from these historical examples which can be applied to church life and pastoral care.

Principles

One immediate principle again is the centrality of prayer—a principle which cannot be emphasised enough. Prayer was at the centre of all that happened in these churches. Another principle is the need for believing prayer coupled with a firm conviction in the ability and willingness of our covenant God to prosper His church and glorify His name. Beddgelert seemed an impossible location for blessing and revival. One Beddgelert church elder, in exhorting an all-age Sunday School in September 1817, quoted an old Welsh hymn, underlining a word in the final line of the hymn which translates as 'from on high'. He applied the phrase effectively: 'Everything of value comes from on high', he affirmed. But also 'from on high comes light, heat and rain; from on high also come blessings of salvation to the earth'. By this time there was considerable power in his words and the attention of all the young and older persons present was rivetted on what he said: 'from the heights also God pours His Holy Spirit... here is hope for the hard men of Beddgelert; if it is dark here, it is light on high; if it is weak here, it is firm and solid on high'. The entire congregation was gripped by conviction of sin and the presence of God filled the church building. The windows of heaven opened with blessing, salvation and joy which then spread like wildfire throughout the parish. Not only was the church changed; the community was transformed and the revival spread for a four-year period over many parts of North Wales.[224]

Are we aware of the power and promises of our living God to bless His people in difficult and seemingly impossible situations? A third principle concerns the need to understand the theology of revival. The same Holy

Spirit who regenerates sinners, convicts of sin, indwells and sanctifies believers, helps in understanding the Bible, quickens in prayer and empowers the preaching of the gospel, is also given to the church in varying degrees of power. There are times when the Lord is more real, the preaching more fruitful and when the church is greatly encouraged. Here is the ongoing or 'ordinary' work of God the Holy Spirit in the church which we dare not despise.

In God's sovereign purpose, however, there are occasions when the Holy Spirit is 'poured' out upon His people and when the preaching becomes extremely powerful and fruitful, impacting the community as well as the church. Do we ignore these differences of degree in the power of the Holy Spirit's ministry or believe the Holy Spirit can work more powerfully in our churches and communities? Whether it is the work of the Holy Spirit in regenerating a sinner or strengthening a believer or working in revival, the difference is one of degree only—there is no qualitative difference. Both are miraculous and supernatural. The difference concerns the intensity and extent of the Holy Spirit's ministry in revival.

Will we seek God for a greater degree and extent of the Holy Spirit's ministry resulting in many conversions with its powerful impact on the church and community? At such times, pastoral care will become even more urgent and necessary.

From historical examples, we turn finally to Romans chapter twelve.

Taking a Church Forward: A Biblical Model

Romans chapter twelve. There are good reasons for concluding our reflection on pastoral care with this chapter.

One reason is that church leaders frequently look for biblical passages to guide them in growing the church spiritually so I offer this chapter for that purpose. A second reason is that Christians often enjoy familiarising themselves with a specific chapter, discussing, sharing, then praying over it in the church, formally and informally. Romans twelve would be extremely rewarding for this purpose. The chapter is also offered because it is comprehensive in addressing major principles touching on Christian discipleship, church life and pastoral care. There is no simplistic solution to the spiritual apathy prevailing within a church or the low level of pastoral care provided. Nevertheless, a church can work responsibly at understanding, relating and praying over the various principles in Romans twelve and find itself growing spiritually in love to the Lord and in mutual care and love for each other.

In addition, Romans chapter twelve is an extremely rich chapter and is 'the largest and most theologically significant of Paul's letters'.[225] There are the redemptive doctrines in chapters 1-11 which are applied from chapter twelve onwards to all members and officers. Romans chapter twelve is also a sample of the apostle's teaching and representative of his applicatory approach in other epistles.

Richard N. Longnecker confirms that the general exhortations and appeals of Romans, including 'the love ethic of a Christian' or church in 12:1-15:13, are 'expressed more expressly and extensively than in any other Pauline New Testament letter.' He emphasises that the general exhortations of chapters 12 and 13 constitute 'an all-encompassing' Christian love ethic which all Christians are called to express 'in all aspects of their lives'.[226] Interestingly, thirty-one of forty-two imperatives in Romans are in this section and a 'good number of imperatival infinitives, adjectives, participles and exhortatory subjunctives are within it as well.'[227] This chapter therefore provides an adequate basis for a pastoral care model. Confirming this, Sinclair Ferguson affirms that the words of Romans 12:1-2 'form the hinge on which Paul's extended exposition of what he calls "my gospel" turns into his detailed practical application of this gospel to personal, social, church and civic life.'[228]

Such a chapter is immediately relevant for our purpose.

Application

I now underline the principles in this chapter and their relevance for church life.

Verses 1-3 are foundational—addressing our relationship to the Lord in terms of wholehearted dedication ('living sacrifices') in the light of God's 'mercies'; consequently there is transformed thinking and a proper estimate of oneself before God and His Word. This is an essential part of the church's response to the Lord, and here are major issues to address in improving pastoral care.

In **verses 4-8,** the unity of the church with its multiplicity of members and gifts is emphasised practically, but a warning is necessary. If believers fail to respond appropriately to the demands of verses 1-3 then their involvement and fellowship in the church will be defective and may harm the church's unity. Difficult or broken relationships within the church and half-hearted commitment can frequently be traced to a faulty relationship with the Lord and a failure to appreciate the wonder of God's grace in Christ.

Verse 9a is a major statement. The thread is God's amazing love in Christ which demands from the church total commitment to the Lord and His church.

From verse 9 there is development—for a general principle is given concerning God-given love expressed practically in **verses 9-21** in relationships within and outside the church. In Greek, verse 9a: 'Let love be without hypocrisy' (ESV: 'Let love be genuine') has the definite article before the noun 'love'— signifying 'the love', most likely pointing to God's love, a love of which He alone is the source.[229]

All our behaviour and relationships are to be governed by 'genuine' love. Haldane refers to the 'hollow words of love',[230] following Calvin's reference to the 'ingenuity' of Christians who give the appearance of love but play-act because their hearts and motives do not correspond with their words. Christians 'ought to throw the mantle of love over the faults of others for Christ's sake'. The relevance of this for church life and pastoral care is striking.

Verses 9-21 teach that love is expressed in obedience and relationships in four ways. **Verses 9-10:** love in action is expressed in two fundamental ways, namely in holy living (v. 9) and in kind, loving and practical attitudes towards others (v. 10). **Verses 11-12** form an intriguing, pastorally sensitive section, including six brief statements directed to maintaining and protecting our relationship with the Lord in key areas.

When Christians are 'lagging in diligence' or backsliding, the apostle directs the church in five steps. 'Fervent in spirit' suggests boiling with passion for the Lord, a reference to the Holy Spirit. Leon Morris adds: 'according to Revelation 3:15, lukewarmness is the worst offence.'[231] 'Serving the Lord' links with verses 1-2 and highlights complete dedication. 'Rejoicing in hope': whatever our circumstances or feelings, the glorious future of Christians can encourage joy in the Lord—it is infectious and encouraging. 'Patient in tribulation', a believing perseverance in all kinds of trials, even in facing death. 'Steadfastly in prayer' (ESV: 'constant in prayer') is the key and where we fail the most.

This triplet of joy in hope, enduring trials and commitment to prayer are basic elements in maintaining our love, zeal and commitment to the Lord. Neglect this directive and we lose out personally and as churches.

Verses 13-16: Love in relationships/situation, includes practical assistance to the needy, hospitality, loving those who persecute and oppose us, rejoicing and weeping with others and thinking humbly and unitedly.

Verses 17-21 continue to provide practical teaching concerning our responses in difficult situations.

Relevance

To illustrate the relevance of this pastoral model for church life, I offer examples from contemporary church life.

Peter

Peter was one of my church elders who had trusted in the Lord Jesus Christ some four years before I met him. He had a lovely Christian wife and two small children. One Sunday morning I preached on the covenant command to 'love the Lord your God with all your heart, with all your soul, with all your mind, and with all your strength' (Matt. 22:37-40; Mark 12:28-34). I was given freedom in preaching. Early afternoon, Peter called to see me. He was under deep conviction, explaining in tears, 'I cannot say I love the Lord with all my heart'. I encouraged him, finally referring to Romans 12:1 where the church is urged to be a 'living sacrifice' in the light of the 'mercies of God'. After prayer he left. To my surprise he returned two hours later. His face shone and as he sat down in my study he exclaimed, 'I can say it now. I love the Lord with all my heart'. Tears of joy flowed down his face as he described the struggles and conviction he had experienced. Reminding him again of the words in Romans 12:1, I shared what one person had said: 'the trouble with a living sacrifice is that it keeps crawling off the altar'!

Peter's love-relationship with the Lord had an enormous impact on other Christians in the church, as he threw himself wholeheartedly into the church's life and pastoral care. This is where the pastoral care model must start because strengthening the unity, spiritual vitality and growth of the church begins, as Peter found, in a wholehearted love to the Lord. Peter's sacrificial care for people flowed genuinely from his deep love for the Lord who had first loved him. That is the source, motive and constraint for authentic pastoral care. Peter has been a spiritual giant in the church caring for people, often sacrificially. Whether struggling with difficult circumstances, or ill, dying or bereaved, Peter could be relied upon to visit them in their homes or hospital. His pastoral care however flowed out of his love relationship with the Lord and his total commitment to the One who had loved and given Himself for him.

Louise and Richard

The next example is different. Louise and Richard[232] belong to different generations with contrasting backgrounds. Working together within the same church often raised problems and disagreements for them. Their personalities were different. Louise is determined and unyielding, always wanting her way. Richard is younger and struggled with working alongside Louise in church activities because of her dominant attitude and harshness. He knew he only pretended to love or respect Louise and his close friends knew that as he gossiped about her. The words of Romans 12:9: 'let love be genuine' hit home hard to him one morning as he read the chapter. He knew his heart was not right. But sadly the situation became impossible, so the pastor became involved in effecting reconciliation. It was not easy but Richard apologised and expressed his desire to continue working alongside Louise in the church. Eventually, Louise agreed and a tense, difficult relationship in the church, with friends taking different sides, was resolved and the church's unity preserved and strengthened.

In the context of Romans twelve, 'to abhor what is evil' meant for Louise and Richard abandoning unkind words/attitudes, gossip and unloving actions. They regretted such attitudes and sought instead to 'cling to what is good' and to please God in their attitudes and words. Such repentance is a grace Christians need to exercise daily and their repentance and desire to please the Lord has encouraged them to care pastorally in genuine ways.

Andrea

Andrea is a single mum struggling to bring up several children despite domestic abuse over a long period by her former husband. Despite court orders protecting her—although too expensive to implement—Andrea continues to suffer psychological, emotional and threatening abuse. The abuse has been horrific with an adverse effect on the children. Remarkably, through all the struggles, pain and tears the Lord has sustained Andrea—giving great grace in the most awful crises.

I link Andrea with Romans chapter twelve as she illustrates its principles well. It is as if she chose this chapter for her life and pastoral model. What I know is that her relationship to the Lord is vibrant and loving with a longing to know and honour Him more. A pastoral concern for all kinds of people is also true of her—whether old or young, ill, bereaved or needy in other ways. She cares for people. Andrea's heart goes out to them with a 'genuine love' and ladies from various backgrounds value her care. Her own personal struggles have become a platform by the Lord's grace to express the principles underlined in Romans twelve. Her deep love of the Lord in appreciation of God's great love in Christ, her desire to be fashioned by the Lord and His Word rather than by the world, with an appropriate estimate of herself, reflect the teaching of verses 1-3 in the chapter.

Andrea is well aware of failures in her local church but attempts to safeguard its unity and support its work. Her 'genuine' love (v. 9, ESV) works at becoming more holy, including being 'kindly affectionate' to her brothers and sisters in Christ. A 'fervent passion' is present also to 'serve the Lord' with a longing to be free to do that increasingly. There is a balance too in her approach. While she struggles with tears and disappointments because of her domestic situation, she has an eternal perspective, enduring tribulation with joy as she anticipates glory ahead.

A dying patient, a bereaved parent or a single mum or an elderly person too infirm to leave the house are among those whom Andrea cares for with a deep love. I submit again that genuine and practical love for the dying, the bereaved and others flows from a person who is deeply in love with the Lord Himself.

Paul

Paul, my former doctoral student, was introduced in an earlier chapter, but I make no apology for referring to him again. He currently serves as a hospice chaplain in the United States. Committed wholeheartedly to the Lord, he had a demanding ministry over a number of years serving churches and seminaries across Eastern Europe. He did valiant work there. Now based in the United States, he has been led into full-time hospice chaplaincy work, and he too is constrained by the love of Christ. Sadly, such work is not rated highly by churches, but I am thrilled he has been given this specific ministry because the needs of people in such places are considerable. Although demanding, Paul is able to be alongside many terminally ill patients and also their distressed and bereaved relatives. I rejoice in this and respect him as exemplifying the principles of Romans twelve in his life and pastoral ministry. Christians need to be alongside the terminally ill and their distressed relatives. In military terms, I view Paul as working in the trenches and engaging in befriending, supporting, loving people who are on the edge of eternity and in need of the gospel of Christ.

None of the individuals referred to above are perfect examples. What I do know is that they mean business with the Lord and want to live by His Word. And it is these individuals, out of love for their Saviour, who are most useful in the ministry of pastoral care. I commend Romans chapter twelve as a pastoral model which may help and challenge you personally and also your church. Churches need to model pastoral care in this radical, God-honouring way.

J. Elwyn Davies

I refer here to a Christian leader in Wales who died in 2007. His name is J. Elwyn Davies who, as a preacher of the gospel and Secretary of the Evangelical Movement of

Wales for thirty-five years, was an outstanding leader and pastor. He embodied the principles delineated in Romans chapter twelve in a striking way. He had fallen deeply in love with the Lord from his conversion and continued in a profoundly intimate relationship with his Saviour throughout his life, living unselfishly for the Lord and His people. His holy life and love for people, even when criticised, is well documented. Alongside his preaching and leadership responsibilities, he had time to care pastorally for Christians, often giving hours of his time to people in need, despite his tiredness.

Idris Charles, a Christian working in the media, testifies: 'I can say that to this day I have never experienced such spiritual company than that of Mr Davies. For me, all that I knew of Jesus Christ radiated through him. His love for me and influence upon me was very great.'[233] Many other people are similarly indebted to Elwyn. His influence was immense.

In 1950, Elwyn's close Christian friend, Celt, was dying in a small hospital in Caernarvon, North Wales. Celt had just completed his training for the Christian ministry and a church in South Wales had invited him to become its pastor. Celt loved the Lord and looked forward to accepting the invitation to pastor the church. At the same time and unexpectedly, however, he was diagnosed as suffering from muscular distrophy (MD), and his condition deteriorated rapidly over the following weeks. No treatment for the disease was known. With others, Elwyn was at his side seeking to support him. When Elwyn asked Celt whether he should accept or refuse the 'call' to pastor a South Wales church, Celt replied, 'I would love to be able to go there', then after a pause he smiled and said, 'I leave it to Him'. Their fellowship together was rich and edifying. The disease developed rapidly and Celt died suddenly one night. Elwyn mourned and missed the fellowship of this dear Christian man. The day after his death, Elwyn stood outside the Caernarvon hospital and watched Celt's coffin being taken home, ready for burial. Unable to speak in that solemn moment, Elwyn had the deep conviction that he would 'have a great deal to do'[234] in giving himself fully to the Lord and continuing the Lord's work which would include, among other things, caring for those dying like Celt. May the Lord raise up more people like Elwyn Davies to care pastorally for people and churches but in the same wise, loving and sacrificial manner. Today, we 'have a great deal to do' pastorally in and through our churches.

Endnotes

1   Although I have written on other subjects, I have written also on aspects of eschatology: *The Wrath of God* (Bridgend, Bryntirion Press, 1984), revised and expanded as *Preaching: An Awesome Task: Wrath, Final Judgement, Hell and the Glorious Gospel* (Bridgend, Bryntirion Press, 2016); *Condemned For Ever!* (Welwyn, Evangelical Press, 1987); *An Angry God? The Biblical Doctrine of Wrath, Final Judgement and Hell* (Bridgend, Bryntirion Press—1991); *Heaven is a Far Better Place:What the Bible Teaches About Heaven* (Darlington, Evangelical Press, 1999).

2   This is pursued in more detail in chapter four.

3   Maesteg (1959-1975) and Bangor (1975-1985).

4   1985-2006 in the Evangelical Theological College of Wales (ETCW), renamed as Wales Evangelical School of Theology (WEST), and expanded in 2016 to become Union School of Theology(UST). Between 2006- 2015, I served as a doctoral Research Supervisor.

5   *Friends of Calvin*, Machiel A. van den Berg (Grand Rapids, Eerdmans, 2009), 132.

6   'The Pornography of Death', Encounter, 1955.

7   *The Revival of Death* (London, Routledge, 1994), 1.

8   *Dying, Death and Grief: a critical biography* (University of Philadelphia Press: 1987).

9   'Modern Death—taboo or not taboo?' (Sociology:25,2:1991), 293-310.

10   *The Revival of Death,* 2.

11   *THE BIG ISSUE*, May 4-10, 2015: 7.

12   This is based on the author's book, *Smoke Gets In Your Eyes* (New York & London: W. W. Norton & Company, Ltd, 2015); also published by Cannongate Books (Edinburgh, 2015).

13   *Being Mortal: Ageing, Illness, Medicine and What Matters in the End* (London, Profile Books, 2014).

14   *Interpreting Death: Christian Theology And Pastoral Practice,* (Eds) Peter C. Jupp and Tony Rogers, (London and Washington, Cassell,1997), xv.

15   E hospice: Palliative Care News: 18 May 2015.

16   'What Good is Thinking About Death?' Flipboard, 29 May 2015.

17   Foreword to Rob Moll's *The Art of Dying: Living Fully into the Life to Come* (Illinois: IVP Books, 2010), 10.

18   'Why we should talk more about death', BBC News Website, 18 May 2012; accessed 2 June 2012.

19   *Being Mortal: Ageing, Illness, Medicine and What Matters in the End* (London, Profile Books, 2014), 1.

20   *Cancer Ward,* Aleksandr Solzhenitsyn (London/New York, Penguin Books, 1971), 152-153.

21   *What Matters In The End: End of Life Care,* Louise Morse (London, Pilgrims' Friend Society, 2016), Back cover. This is a small but extremely useful and practical book which merits a wide readership.

22   *Living Out God's Purpose in our Senior Years: Developing Usefulness in Old Age*, Louise Morse and Roger Hitchings (London, Pilgrims' friend Society, 2014). A small, practical book with biblical principles which is worth reading.

23   *The Art of Dying: Living Fully into the Life to Come* (Downers Grove, Illinois; IVP Books, 2010), 151.

24   *Finishing Our Course with Joy: Ageing With Hope*, J. I. Packer (Nottingham/Wheaton, IVP/Crossway, 2014), 74-75.

25   *Professor of Philosophy at Wright State University in Dayton, Ohio.*

26   *A Guide To The Good Life: the Ancient Art of Stoic Joy* (Oxford: Oxford University Press, 2009).

27   Quoted by Julie Beck in 'What Good is Thinking about Death?' (The Atlantic Monthly Group; 28 May 2015), 32.

28   'What Good is Thinking about Death?', 35.

29   *The Revival of Death,* Tony Walter: inside page.

30   *The Revival of Death,* 5.

31   *The Revival of Death,* 5; see also 47-65.

32   *Interpreting Death,* xv-xvi.

33   *The Life of Alfred Hitchcock,* Donald Spoto (London: Collins, 1983), 552.

34   Dying grace and the subject of assurance in dying are dealt with in more detail in chapter four.

35   Charles Hodge, for example, uses this phrase in his *Princeton Sermons* (Edinburgh, Banner of Truth Trust, 1958), 356.

36   *Being Mortal,* 6-7.

37   *The Physicians's Covenant: Images of the Healer in Medical Ethics* (Philadelphia, Westminster Prress, 1983), 32-34.

38   *The Physician's Covenant,* 44.

39   This Oath, named after Hippocrates, a Greek philosopher/physician living between 466 -377 B.C, emerged a century later with no certainty as to the author/s.

40   Euthanasia/medically assisted dying are referred to in a later chapter.

41   *Being Mortal,* 69.

42   *The Christian Art of Dying: Learning from Jesus* (Cambridge/Grand Rapids: Eerdmans, 2011), 3.

43   'Communication and awareness about death: A study of a random sample of dying people', Clive Seale: Social Science & Medicine: Volume 32, Issue 8, 1991:943-952.

44   *Attitudes to Ageing and Dying* (Peniel, Carmarthen: Powell Charity Trust, 2013), 73.

45   'Death, technology, and Gender in Postmodern American Society', Jeanne Quint Benoliel in *Death and The Quest for Meaning,* Stephen Strack (ed), (Northvale, New Jersey/London, Jason Aronson Inc, 1997), 40.

46   *Limits to Medicine: medical nemesis: the expropriation of health,* Ivan Illich (London: Marian Boyars, 1976).

47   '...the healer had to acknowledge his limits. At such a moment, withdrawal was the proper service a physician rendered to his patient's good death': Ivan Illich, The Aisling Magazine, Issue 19, 1996.

48   Ivan Illich would have had a different view.

49   This example may illustrate what Illich recognised later in 1995 as 'the result of an even more sinister reality' in which medicine like education became 'organised as systems'.

50   'Death Undefeated: From medicine to medicalisation to systematisation', *The Aisling Magazine*, Issue 19, Bealtaine 1996.

51   This is one of the largest British charities. Established in 1911 the charity aims to provide specialist health and social care, information and financial support to people affected by cancer. An important priority for the charity is to obtain better cancer care.

52   *The Christian Art of Dying: Learning from Jesus,*23.

53   A slippery term and, as we have seen, used critically. Care is needed in understanding the term.

54   1918-2005. Saunders was a nurse then a social worker who later studied medicine in London at the age of thirty-three followed by a period of medical research into pain management. An agnostic for some years, she professed the Christian faith when holidaying with Christian friends in Cornwall. She said it was 'as if a switch had flipped' and she believed.

55   Florence Wald took a sabbatical from Yale in 1968 to work in St Christopher's in London in order to learn as much as possible from Saunders. Along with a couple of paediatricians and a chaplain, Wald founded Connecticut Hospice in Branford, Connecticut in 1974.

56   'Policy and the Re-Formation of Hospice: Lessons from the Past for the Future of Palliative Care', Joy Buck, HHS Public Access, 2011 Nov-Dec:13 (6): S36-S43.

57   See www. stchristophers.org.uk/abouthistory

58   *Cicely Saunders —Founder of the Hospice Movement. Selected Letters 1959-1999*, Clark D, ed (Oxford University Press, 2002). The editor chose 700 out of about 7,000 of her letters for his narrative. A wide range of subjects are covered with valuable insights.

59   The term 'palliative care' was proposed in 1974 by a Canadian surgeon, Balfour Mount. This term is not identical with terminal/end of life care for the latter simply provides relief.

60   'Dame Cicely Saunders: Founder of the Modern Hospice Movement', Caroline Richmond, *British Medical Journal*, July 23, 2005.

61   'Hospice's Path to the Future' in *Death and the Quest for Meaning*, 57.

62   Joy Buck, 'Policy and the Re-Formation of Hospice: Lessons from the past for the Future of Palliative Care', 2011 Nov-Dec:13 (6): 535-543; HHS Public Access.

63   *Being Mortal*, 193.

64   *Death and the Quest for Meaning*, 57-58.

65   Awareness of Dying: An experience of Chinese Patients with Terminal Cancer in OMEGA—*Journal of Death and Dying*, vol. 43, No.3/2001, 259-279.

66   *On Death and Dying* (New York, Macmillan, 1969).

67   *The Meaning of Death* (New York, McGraw-Hill, 1959).

68   *The Dying Patient* (New York, Russell Sage Foundation, 1970). Interestingly, this book also has a valuable bibliography covering over 300 publications between 1955-1970 dealing with the topic of dying.

69   *Death and the Quest for Meaning*, 329-330.

70   'Introduction: A Personal Memoir of Herman Feifel', Charles Ansell in *Death and the Quest for Meaning*, Stephen Strack, editor, (New Jersey/London, Jason Aronson Inc, 1997), xxv.

71   Lucy Bregman also refers to these examples in her *Preaching Death*, 114.

72   *Preaching Death: The Transformation of Christian Funeral Sermons*, Lucy Bregman (Waco, Texas, Baylor University Press, 2011), 6.

73   *The Art of Ministering to the Sick*, R.C. Cabot and R.L. Dicks, (New York/London, Macmillan, 1936).

74   Communication and awareness about dying in the 1990s, David Field and Gina Copp, *Palliative Medicine*, vol.13, No.6, 459-468.

75   Journal of Oncology Practice, May 2008, Vol.4.No.3, 153-157.

76   One example is the Liverpool Care Pathway (LCP). The Liverpool University Hospital and Liverpool Marie Curie Hospital reviewed their care of those patients in the final stages of dying. Consequently, by 2010 the Liverpool Palliative Care Institute published a summary of their guidelines for care workers, urging their use more widely. The Department of Health approved the Guidelines and by now many hospitals in the UK have adopted them. However, despite success, there have been complaints; for example, a failure to inform patients and families, an over dependence on sedation and withdrawal of water and food, even when requested by the patient thus hastening death.

77   'Between hope and acceptance: the medicalisation of dying', BMJ April, 324, (7342): 905-907.

78   *Attitudes to Ageing and Dying*, 97.

79   *Joni,* Joni Eareckson (London/Glasgow, Zondervan/Pickering & Inglis, 1978).

80   *The Scars That Have Shaped Me: How God Meets Us In Suffering*, Vaneetha Rendall Risner (Minneapolis, Desiring God, 2016), 26.

81   *Joni*, 206.

82   *Joni,* 148.

83   *Joni*, 88.

84   *The Scars That Have Shaped Me*, 12.

85   *The Scars That Have Shaped Me*, 54.

86   *Joni,* 82.

87   *Confessions,* 1.1, (Grand Rapids, M1, Christian Classics Library, 1999), 17.

88   *Reasons For The Christian Hope*, (Fearn, Christian Focus, 2009), 34.

89   *The Shorter Catechism with Scripture Proofs* (Edinburgh/Carlisle, Pennsylvania, Banner of Truth, nd), 1.

90   *Joni*, 112.

91   Interestingly, the Heidelberg Catechism poses a related question to that asked by Joni:' **Q:**Since Christ has died for us, why do we still have to die? **A.** Our death is not a payment for our sins, but it puts an end to sin and is an entrance into eternal life'. *Living and Dying in Joy: A Devotional Guide to the Heidelberg Catechism,* Cornelis Vonk (Grand Rapids, Paideia Press, 2013), 92.

92   *Ryle's Expository Thoughts on the Gospels,* J. C. Ryle (Grand Rapids, Zondervan, n.d), 180.

93   *The Scars That Have Shaped Me*, 21-23.

94   A pseudonym as this lady prefers to remain anonymous. I am grateful to her for providing, through a mutual friend, a detailed account of her experiences.

95   *A Grief Observed,* (London, Faber & Faber, 1961), 7.

96   *The Scars That Have Shaped Me,* 77-80.

97   *Choices Changes*, Joni Eareckson Tada (Grand Rapids/Basingstoke, Zondervan/Pickering and Inglis,1986), 81-82.

98   *Living and Dying in Joy: A Devotional Guide to the Heidelberg Catechism*, 63.

99   *HELLO? Is Anyone There? A Pastoral Reflection on the Struggle with 'Unanswered' Prayer,* Roger Philip Abbott (Eugene, Oregon, Cascade Books, Wipf & Stock, 2014), 106-112.

100   *Joni*, 48.

101   For different reasons, Friederich Nietzsche (1844-1900), a German philologist and philosopher in a well known statement declared: 'In a certain state it is indecent to live longer. To go on vegetating in cowardly dependence on physicians and machinations, after the meaning of life, the right to life has been lost, that ought to prompt a profound contempt in society...I want to die proudly when it is no longer possible to live proudly': A Primer in Bioethics (2nd edition), G. Meilaender, (Grand Rapids, Eerdmans, 2005), 98.

102   *Joni*, 50-51.

103   *Diamonds in the Dust,* Jon Eareckson Tada (London, Marshall & Pickering, 1993), 14.

104   Helpful resources include the British Association of Counselling & Psychotherapy (BACP) on Working with Suicidal Clients. Among other things, they refer to the risk factors (p.9) and factors that can make suicide less likely (p.10). Readers may also be interested to refer to the Welsh Assembly National Action Plan to Reduce Suicide and Self-Harm in Wales 2009-2014.

105   International Association for Suicide Prevention. They add: 'It usually occurs gradually, progressing from suicidal thoughts, to planning, to attempting suicide and finally dying by suicide'.

106   Mowat Research and Centre for Spirituality, Health and Disability, University of Aberdeen, 2008

107   *The Way of Blessing: Stepping into the Presence and Mission of God,* Roy Godwin (Colorado Springs/Eastbourne, David Cook, Kingsway, 2016), Chapter Two. A critical reading of this book is required.

108   Rob Marris, Labour M.P for Wolverhampton introduced a Private Member's Bill in June 2015. This was heavily defeated in the House of Commons in September 2015.

109   *The Times*, 31 March 2008

110   *Is There A Christian Case For Assisted Dying? Voluntary Euthanasia Reassessed*, (London, S.P.C.K, 2009).

111   *Christian Ethics and Moral Problems,* W. R. Inge, (London, Hodder & Stoughton, 1930), 373.

112   *On Dying Well: A Contribution to the Euthanasia Debate*, Second edition, (London, Church House Publishing, 2000), 20.

113   See for example *Is There A Christian Case For Assisted Dying: Voluntary Euthanasia Reassessed,* Paul Badham (London, S.P.C.K, 2007), chapter three. Also *Matters of Life and Death, chapter nine.*

114   *On Dying Well: A Contribution to the Euthanasia Debate,* xi.

115   *On Dying Well,* second edition, ix-x.

116   *One Minute After You Die*, Erwin Lutzer (Chicago, Moody Press, 1997), 79.

117   *On Dying Well,* 15.

118   I am indebted to Steffan Job, staff worker with the Evangelical Movement of Wales who has devised this approach to reach unbelievers in the National Eisteddfod in Wales (August 2017).

119   A similar but possibly more stark and challenging novel is A. I. Solzhenitsyn's, *Cancer Ward* (London/New York, Penguin Books, 1971).

120   *The Complete Psychological Works of Sigmund Freud* (London, 1957, volume 14), 289.

121   Daily Mail Online, Wednesday 5 August 2015.

122   *Dem Dry Bones: Preaching, Death and Hope*, Luke A. Powery (Minneapolis, Fortress Press, 2012), 10.

123   Three different words are translated as 'hell' in the Authorized Version of the Bible. The Hebrew word *Sheol* and the Greek *Hades* refer either to the grave or the state of death but also on a few occasions to the state of unbelievers in hell (for example, Luke 16:23). The Greek word *Gehenna* describes the abode and punishment of unbelievers in hell especially after the Final Judgment.

124   See the relevant section in chapter six indicating how the Lord Jesus handled the doctrine of hell in His own ministry on earth. Also *The Nature of Hell: A Report by the Evangelical Alliance Commission on Unity and Truth Among Evangelicals (ACUTE)*, Carlisle, ACUTE/Paternoster, 2000), 118-120.

125   Email correspondence with Dr Paul Held 28 January 2017.

126   *Dementia: Living in the Memories of God,* John Swinton, (Grand Rapids/ Cambridge, Eerdmans, 2012), 58-59.

127   *Dementia*, 85-86.

128   In her valuable but small book on *Caring For An Elderly Parent: When Grandma Comes To Stay* (London, Pilgrims' friend Society, 2016), Sarah Jones, a medical physician with family and professional experience in this area, refers to the help that caregivers at home require as: 1) spiritual—prayer, fellowship, helping practically as a church, enabling the carer to attend church, 2) emotional, being available to chat to the carer, etc, 3) physical—making meals, giving lifts if necessary, collecting medicines, relieving the carer, ii.

129   All these quotations are from Dr Paul Held's email on 28 January 2017.

130   Email correspondence 10 May 2017.

131 *Sunsets: Reflections for Life's Final Journey,* Deborah Howard (Wheaton, Crossway Books, 2005), 15.

132 *Sunsets*, 124.

133 *Sunsets*, 16.

134 For several brief, historical accounts of believers dying, see my *Heaven is a Far Better Place: What the Bible teaches about Heaven* (Darlington, Evangelical Press, 1999), 201-205.

135 *Westminster Confession of Faith*, 18:1.

136 *Princeton Sermons: Outlines of Discourses, Doctrinal and Practical* (London, Banner of Truth, 1958), 350.

137 Series, *Taste and See* Articles, August 28, 1998.

138 'A Sermon On Preparing To Die,' 1519, *Luther's Works: Devotional Writings* 1, Vol 42, Martin O. Dietrich, editor, (Philadelphia, Fortress Press, 1969), 99-114.

139 *Pilgrim's Progress,* John Bunyan (Edinburgh, Banner of Truth, 1977), 180-188.

140 *How Long, O Lord? Reflections on Suffering & Evil*, D.A. Carson (Leicester, IVP/Baker, 1990), 148

141 *New Testament Theology*, Donald Guthrie (Leicester, IVP. 1981), 879. Other New Testament scholars also agree. See, for example: *The Gospel According to John,* D. A. Carson (Grand Rapids/Leicester, IVP/Eerdmans, 1991),488-9; *The Gospel of John,* W. Hendriksen (London, Banner of Truth,1959), 265; *The Gospel According to St.John: An Introduction and Commentary,* R.V.G Tasker (London, Tyndale/IVP, 1960), 171.

142 *The Epistles of Paul to the Thessalonians: an introduction and commentary*, Leon Morris (London, Tyndale/IVP, 1956), 89.

143 'Eschatology', *Cambridge Companion to Christian Doctrine*, Colin E. Gunton, ed:(Cambridge, Cambridge University Press,1997), 226.

144 *The Hope of the Early Church,* Brian E. Daly (Cambridge, Cambridge University Press, 1991), 2.

145 *Systematic Theology*, L. Berkhof (Edinburgh, Banner of Truth Trust, 1959), 666-667.

146 *Systematic Theology: An Introduction to Biblical Doctrine* (IVP/Zondervan, Leicester/Grand Rapids, 1994), 1091.

147 *God, Revelation and Authority* (Brooklyn, Word Books, 1976).

148 *Surprised by Hope*, Tom Wright (London, SPCK, 2007), 183-184.

149 *Surprised by Hope*, 210.

150 *Cambridge Companion to Christian Doctrine,* 226.

151 The Scottish Bulletin of Evangelical Theology, W.C. Campbell-Jack, Vol.7, no.2, 120.

152 Chapter XXX; Section 111.

153   *The Church and the Last Things,* Dr Martyn Lloyd-Jones (London, Hodder & Stoughton, 1997), Volume 3, 93-94.

154   *The Confession of Faith: A Handbook of Christian Doctrine Expounding The Westminster Confession*, A.A. Hodge (London/Edinburgh, Banner of Truth Trust, 1958), 395-396.

155   *The Puritan Hope*, Iain Murray (Edinburgh, Banner of Truth, 1971), 141.

156   *New Life In The Wasteland: 2 Corinthians on the Cost and Glory of the Christian Ministry*, Douglas F. Kelly (Fearn/Edinburgh, Christian Focus and Rutherford House, 2003), 104-105.

157   *The Hope of the Early Church,* Brian E. Daly (Cambridge, Cambridge University Press, 1991), 2.

158   *Living and Dying in Joy: A Devotional Guide to the Heidelberg Catechism*, 110.

159   'The Context of Funeral Ministry Today', *Interpreting Death: Christian Theology and Pastoral Practice,* edited by Peter C. Jupp and Tony Rogers (London and Washington, Cassell, 1997), 11.

160   *Interpreting Death: Christian Theology and Pastoral Practice,* 10-14.

161   First published in hard -back in 1975 by J.B. Lippincott, USA.

162   Nashville, Tenn; Abingdon Press, 1966.

163   The Times Newspaper, Friday, March 18, 2016.

164   Originally established in Australia in 1975.

165   There is an NOCN Accredited Syllabus which is recognised by the UK Government. A Level 3 Certificate in 'Civil Celebrancy in the United Kingdom' (QCF) is available as well as a Diploma Course.

166   *Accompany Them With Singing: The Christian Funeral,* Thomas G. Long (Louisville, Kentucky, Westminster John Knox Press, 2013), xv.

167   *Accompany Them With Singing*, 7.

168   *Accompany Them With Singing*, 183.

169   *Interpreting Death: Christian Theology and Pastoral Practice,* Peter C. Jupp and Tony Rogers, editors (London and Washington, Cassell, 1997), 144.

170   *Interpreting Death*, 89.

171   'The Needs of Bereaved People at the Time of the Funeral' in *Interpreting Death: Christian Theology and Pastoral Practice,* 89.

172   'To be Dead is Not Enough', in *Interpreting Death: Christian Theology and Pastoral Practice*, 34.

173   *A Matter of Life and Death: Preaching at Funerals* (Cambridge, Massachusetts, Cowley Publications, 2002), 3.

174   *The Drama of Doctrine: A Canonical Linguistic Approach to Christian Theology* (Louisville, Kentucky, Westminster John Knox Press, 2005),

175   *The Drama of Doctrine*, 35.

176 *Truth Decay: Defending Christianity Against the Challenges of Postmodernism,* Douglas Groothuis (Illinois/Leicester, 2000), 22.

177 *The Death of Truth,* Dennis McCallum, General Editor (Minneapolis, Minnesota, Bethany House Publishers, 1996), 249.

178 *Commentary on the Book of the Prophet Isaiah:* Volume 4, trans. William Pringle (Edinburgh: Calvin Translation Society, 1854), 172.

179 Sermons on Deuteronomy, John Calvin, trans. Arthur Golding (Edinburgh, Banner of Truth Trust, 1987), 1206.

180 *Isaiah,* John Calvin, Volume 4.61.

181 *A Matter of Life and Death: Preaching at Funerals,* Charles Hoffacker (Cambridge, Massachusetts, Cowley Publications, 2002), 17. I am indebted to this author for stimulating me in reflecting further on the issue.

182 It was interesting reading *Dem Dry Bones: Preaching, Death, and Hope,* Luke A. Powery (Minneapolis, Fortress Press, 2012). Rejecting Prosperity teaching which he describes as 'Candy' theology, Powery sees it as flawed partly because of 'its attempt to proclaim hope while avoiding or denying death' (6). He uses the African/American spirituals as a resource and key for understanding the Christian hope in contemporary American society.

183 *An Exposition of Ezekiel* (Grand Rapids, Sovereign Grace Publishers, 1971), 23. See my *Preaching—An Awesome Task: Wrath, Final Judgement, Hell and the Glorious Gospel* (Bridgend, Bryntirion Press, 2016).

184 *Brothers, We Are Not Professionals: A Plea For Radical Ministry* (Fearn, Ross-shire, Christian Focus Publications, 2003), 4.

185 *Preaching & Preachers* (London, Hodder and Stoughton, 1971), 88.

186 *The Christian Art of Dying: Learning from Jesus,* Allen Verhey, 349.

187 Director of Research and Professor of Systematic and Historical Theology, Union School of Theology (Ust), Bridgend,Wales and Oxford).

188 Email, 17 April, 2015.

189 *Dr. Martyn Lloyd-Jones And Evangelicals in Wales: Bala Ministers' Conference 1955-2014,* D.Eryl Davies, (Bridgend, Wales, Bryntirion Press, 2014).

190 *A Grief Observed*, C. S. Lewis (London, Faber and Faber, 1961).

191 *A Grief Observed,* see pages 5-17 for the quotations which follow.

192 *A Grief Observed,* 38-39.

193 *A Grief Observed,* 40.

194 *A Grief Observed,* 50.

195 *Interpreting Death: Christian Theology and Pastoral Practice*, Peter C. Jupp and Tony Rogers (editors), 120-129 (London and Washington, Cassell, 1997).

196 *The Times*, Thursday 9 July 2015.

197 'Grief and Bereavement Theories', *Nursing Standard*, 24,41.44-47, 2010.

198 *Grief: Living at Peace with Loss,* June Hunt (Torrance, California, Aspire Press, 2013), 12-14.

199   *Grief: Living at Peace with Loss*, 27-28, 61.

200   *On Death and Dying,* Elisabeth Kubler-Ross (New York/London, Macmillan, 1969).

201   *The Revival of Death*, 70.

202   'Living Around Grief', Bereaved Parents Together (BPT). Adapted by Mel Phelps (Jan 2010) from Lois Tonkin, Grief Counsellor, Wellington, New Zealand.

203   *Attachment and Loss: Separation, Anxiety and Anger,* J, Bowlby, Vol. 11, (London, Hogarth Press, 1973).

204   'Supporting the Bereaved: Theory and Practice', Ann Dent, *Counselling at Work,* Autumn 2005, 22.

205   *Supporting the Bereaved: Theory and Practice*, 23.

206   *The Gospel According to John,* D. A. Carson (Grand Rapids/Leicester, Eerdmans/IVP, 1991), 415-416.

207   B. B. Warfield, 'The Emotional Life of Our Lord' in *The Person and Work of Christ* (Presbyterian and Reformed, 1950), 115.

208   A useful and stimulating discussion of this subject, including 'The Language of Leadership', is found in *The People's Theologian: Writings in Honour of Donald Macleod,* ed. I.D Campbell & Malcom Maclean (Fearn, Christian Focus, 2011), 265-288.

209   *The People's Theologian,* 285.

210   *Devoted To God: Blueprints for Sanctification*, Sinclair B. Ferguson (Edinburgh, Banner of Truth, 2016), 29.

211   *The Hole In Our Holiness: Filling the Gap Between Gospel Passion and the Pursuit of Godliness,* Kevin DeYoung (Wheaton, Crossway, 2012), 21.

212   *The Hole In Our Holiness*, 38-47.

213   *Breakout Churches: Discover How to Make the Leap*, Thom S. Rainer (Grand Rapids, Zondervan, 2005).

214   Recorded in the Congressional Board of the Proceedings and debates of the 108th Congress, First Session, 30-9-2003. On this date, the House of Representatives paid tribute to him for his outstanding church ministry and contribution to society.

215   *Pastoral Leadership,* 101.

216   *Pastoral Leadership: A Case Study, including Reference to John Chrysostom,* Won Sang Lee *(*Eugene, Oregon, Wipf & Stock, 2015), 67.

217   *Pastoral Leadership,* 83, 88-91.

218   *The Spectator*, 13 June 2015

219   *The Freedom of Self-Forgetfulness: The Path to True Christian Joy,* Timothy Keller (Farington, Leyland, England, 10 Publishing, 2012).

220   *The Freedom of Self-Forgetfulness,*33-36, 42.

221   Literally: 'Chapel by the stream'.

222   *The Instructor* or in Welsh *Y Hyfforddwr,* was published in 1807. Its author, Thomas Charles (1755-1814), was ordained as an Anglican curate but had embraced Calvinistic theology. It was not long before he joined the Calvinistic Methodists as a preacher, contributing significantly to the Lord's work in Wales. He was based in Bala, North Wales and later became involved in founding the Bible Society in London.

223   A small farm house under the shadow of Snowdon called Hafod-y-Llan. The old farm house has been preserved by the National Trust and is available for viewing.

224   A more detailed account is provided in *The Beddgelert Revival,* Eryl Davies (Bridgend, Bryntirion Press,2004).

225   *An Introduction To The New Testament,* D. A. Carson, Douglas J. Moo and Leon Morris (Grand Rapids, Zondervan, 1992), 239.

226   *The Epistle to the Romans: A Commentary on the Greek Text* (NIGTC), Richard N. Longenecker (Grand Rapids, Eerdmans, 2016), 912.

227   *Paul's Letters to the Romans; A Commentary* (Grand Rapids/Cambridge, UK, Eerdmans, 2011), 435.

228   *Devoted to God: Blueprints For Sanctification,* Sinclair B. Ferguson (Edinburgh, Banner of Truth, 2016), 32.

229   *The Epistle to the Romans,* 936-937. Longenecker confirms that Paul may be 'making the point that what he is talking about here is God's love as expressed in and through the life of a Christian' and a church.

230   *Exposition of the Epistle to the Romans*, Robert Haldane (London, Banner of Truth, 1958), 563-564.

231   *The Epistle to the Romans,* 446.

232   These names and the following ones are changed to ensure anonymity.

233   'Introduction', by Eryl Davies in *A Father In The Faith: J.Elwyn Davies, 1925-2007,* John Emyr (ed), (Bridgend, Bryntirion Press, 2012), 25.

234   An article by Elwyn Davies 'Remembering Celt', in *A Father in the Faith*, 123-127. See also the original Welsh language book, *Porth yr Aur: Cofio J. Elwyn Davies,* Golygwyd gan John Emyr (Pen-y-bont, Gwasg Bryntirion, 2011), 117-121.